PIERA
A True Story of Love and Survival in World War II Italy

By Piera Salvatici Misciattelli Bernardini

1950: Leaving Rocca Di Papa For Sardinia

Early life from 1933 birth and departure for Greece

1936: Departure for Rhodes

Life in Cremasto on the island of Rhodes

1938: The town of Trianda on Rhodes

The city of Rhodes

School performance

Rhodes and the ship of refugee Jews

The winds of war arrive in Rhodes

Departure from Rhodes

Disembarkation and train to Italy

1942: Venice and Re-entry into Tuscany

Departure for Bertinoro in Emilia Romagna

1943: Arrival Bertinoro

To my parents and to my siblings
Because I grew up with them.
To my children
Dona, Dani, Momi, Igo.
And to their father Gregorio
Always and forever with me

With unbounded love,
Mamma

"It is said: in the end you are all that which you have pondered, loved, accomplished.

I would add: you are that which you remember.

Memories are a treasure for you, more than the sentiments that you fostered, the thoughts you have thought, the actions you have accomplished, these memories that you have preserved and have not let fade away, and of which you remained the only custodian...

May you let yourself live until the memories do not abandon you and that you may, in your turn, abandon yourself in them."

-    N. Bobbi

1950: LEAVING ROCCA DI PAPA FOR SARDINIA

My gaze was lost in the distance as I tried to make out the town of Rocca di Papa, to imprint in my mind that which I was leaving, possibly forever.

I watched as the airplane taxied down the runway of the Frosinone airport. Taxied is perhaps an exaggerated word for what the plane was doing. It was an old military plane, perhaps even on its last flight, extremely rickety.

But there it stood against the blue sky, proud of its appearance, haughty in its insignia and past glories. The plane gave a sudden start in a chorus of suspicious and deafening roars.

"Slowly, Pilot...I beg you...more slowly," I thought.

My heart implored that the old relic wouldn't be able to take the flight, but this hope was a pipedream. The rational part of me had an absolute certainty that my parents would never have given up on heading to our new destination, with its promise of new experiences and expectations they believed would be better for us. My life had been a succession of departures, followed by stays some long and some short. Then more departures, only to be followed by more new arrivals.

The airplane was by now very close to us and my suffering became even deeper. "Be strong, Piera, smile!," I consoled myself.

I was little more than 17 years old and I was leaving Rocca di Papa, my home and my whole world for the last three years. I was leaving the friends I had attained with great difficulty, I was leaving the thick forests and paths we walked, above a panorama that took our breath away for how beautiful it was.

I was leaving everything that I loved: Monte Cavo, said to be the old road traveled by the Egyptian queen Cleopatra with all of her entourage. I was leaving behind the long walks at the legendary Madonna of the Rock.

"Please, little Madonna, you who stopped that huge rock from falling and killing the knight from certain death...I implore you to let me remain here for all of my life..."

I was leaving Lake Albano, dark and mysterious. The forests which flaunted in every season a thousand variations of greens, sometimes dark, sometimes tender and brilliant.
We used to walk in autumn on those soft carpets of leaves that at every step seemed to complain with a crunch that was sad and at the same time serene.

And in the evening, in the distance, we would look from afar and see Rome, mythical and one in a million, with its thousands upon thousands of lights that challenged the beauty even of the starred sky. Our gaze would be entranced and even confused by that eternal competition. Rome was there, you could almost touch her, and you almost felt as if she, Rome, were your own creation.

If my parents had lived in pioneer times, they surely would have owned a carriage. Today the means of transportation have changed of course. There is the train, the ship, the plane. My parents remained fixed in time, always the same: for them, the essence of existence was that roots should never have time to cling to the earth. Nomads in search of novelty, always bored with what they had already experienced, they were constantly propelled by a desire for the unknown of the future.

My interaction with the little Madonna of the Rock had now faded, and we were all seated inside the airplane. I found myself hoping that everything would go well considering the battered conditions of this leftover remnant of war. The engines whirled at maximum capability, the metal plates of the fuselage focused on their determination to hold themselves together.

Skepticism was apparent on Mamma's face, but Papa smiled. I think he was the only one who would have wagered that that airplane could fly. With a final push and a mix of pride and dignity - together with a unified gasp of all the passengers - the airplane took off into the air, majestic and cognizant of its past glories.

Mamma was reassuring my sister Brunella, holding her tightly to her chest. Papà spoke with Attico, my big brother, and explained that he himself had repaired this airplane, while Attico looked at him with admiration. Franco, the third of my siblings in order of age, held close a shoebox whose lid was peppered with tiny air holes.

On the inside of this box were two tiny greenfinches, baby birds that had fallen from their nest. He had saved them, feeding them every two hours with cookies and milk. He grasped tightly this precious treasure. It was difficult to know what he was thinking. Perhaps his explorations through the bushes of Scotch broom, or about the fort he would repeatedly build and then demolish, always certain that he could make it better.

Brunella was too little, her emotions clouding the excitement of her first flight.

I looked at them. Why were they happy and I was not? I would have liked at least to be calm, and assuage my regrets in the beauty of the sky and the blue of the sea. But the distance of Rocca di Papa seemed infinite and the return ever more impossible.

I thought about when we had first arrived at Rocca di Papa, in 1947. At that time we were coming from Bertinoro, a little town in Emilia Romagna. I think about the respect and trust of the townspeople of Rocca di Papa, respect and trust which we won with difficulty. It was a struggle to make friends in those new environs. And at all costs we wanted to make new friends.

The war had made everyone more suspicious and egoistic. It threw light on the negative aspects of each person, like racism, a deplorable sentiment but innate in every human being.

It is easier and safer to suspect someone than to try to understand them.

What family is this? Where are they from? Are they respectable people?

And in their suspicion, they insinuate things between one question and another. Certainly, if we were a respectable family, we would have our own town and our own house. It was 1947, and everyone who had left their hometown inevitably was a fugitive, a refugee, or to be direct, a suspect.

In reality, we seemed to be a normal family. A bit vagabond but normal, a family like so many others.

Only now do I realize how exceptional my parents were: always ready for new experiences, inclined to adapt to the customs and dress of various places, trailblazing a way of life very different from the normal routine. They did not want to live and die in the same place. They were devoted and steadfast in the fundamental basics of upbringing children, a sense of duty and deep love and respect for our magnificent country, Italy. For my parents nothing was greater than the desire to see what was on the other side of the hills. And no hill was identical to another.

We were in flight between heaven and sea...but I could still feel on my face the fresh fragrance of the Scotch broom of Rocca di

Papa, its perfume, it's caresses...I was daydreaming, but my tears were real.

EARLY LIFE FROM 1933 BIRTH AND DEPARTURE FOR GREECE

"The things that the child adores
Remain in the kingdom of the heart
All the way into old age
The most beautiful thing about life
Is that our soul remains
fluttering in the places where
Once we played"

- K. Gibran

I closed my eyes and began to unroll the thread of my life so far.

I was born in Orbetello, a little town in Tuscany at the border of sky and sea. It was April 1 of 1933.

In Orbetello, at the time of my birth, they were preparing for one of the very first transatlantic flights. I imagine that the people there at the time were experiencing an atmosphere of enthusiastic pride. [1] Italy was savoring its most beautiful years, very aware of being a great nation, swelling with glory and with pride.

And there I was born, a little tessera in a mosaic of people who deluded themselves into thinking that they were unique and one in a million.

I am not a direct witness of the first moves my parents made around the Italian peninsula, between Rome and Milan. My world was then in the niche between my mother's arms.

Until: Destination Lero, a little island in the Aegean sea. This is the first important trip of which I remember. We embarked at Brindisi on the southeastern coast of Italy.

My brother Attico was five years old and I was two. He was absolutely convinced that my parents had bought me so that he wouldn't be alone. I was his, and his protection was constant and meticulous. He helped me go down the stairs, he buttoned my jacket so that I wouldn't catch cold, and he ensured that there weren't any rocks too big for my little feet. He loved me as one loves something absolute and precious. I was little, but the memories are indelible; they are a part of me.

The island of Lero lay in an incredible turquoise sea and our house stood out against the sky. The house was sheltered between rocks which were eroding towards the sea. It was a white house, white as if to challenge the exuberance of the various shades of blue. Better said, the walls were a brilliant white while the floors and windows were blue. I remember a large terrace and Attico's hand rested on my shoulder, as if to hold me back from the rocks that tumbled into the sea.

Little tufts of vegetation almost afraid to exist protruded from the rocks, and far below was a bay of a certain blue more intense than the mind can possibly imagine.

It was there that they conducted the military parades. Young men upright in their immaculate uniforms, with their proud gaze towards the sea and their hearts brimming with anticipation.

How many of them ever returned? How many will have been able to relive that moment?

The seaplanes rumbled between the sky and the sea like butterflies, ready to adorn Italy in pride and well deserved glory.

I can smell the sea and feel the wind frolicking in my hair. I don't want to forget. I want to see, to imprint in my mind the vision of my mother on the pier, her hand holding on to her hat, a battle she almost always lost. On the island of Leros, the wind does not permit missteps; it always wins.

Mamma was taking off her hat and concentrating all of her efforts now on her dress, which, clinging to her body, created a harmonious and amusing waving effect. Perhaps the wind wanted to show off the feminine form of my mother.

She was plumpish, with pale and luminous skin, and a mouth with the most dazzling smile I can recall. For years I attempted to imitate that smile with the delusion that I could be like her. Mamma's golden hair sparkled like pyrite, a mineral that they used to mine in Gavorrano, the hometown of my parents. The wind caressed her hair and made her curls dance, giving off sparks of gold. Her eyes were jade green. Nature had graced her with all of its generosity.

I closed my eyes and relived those moments. I thank God for my memory. Now that I have so little, it is what I live for.

1936: DEPARTURE FOR RHODES

Lero was a lovely but brief period. After a little while, we returned for a few months to Italy, where we had a few other stays not worthy of much mention.

And then the great event.

I remember that Papà came home after work. With a sense of achievement in his stride and breeze in his tufts of hair, he led Mamma in a whirling dance around our little kitchen table. I squeezed Attico's hand, which seemed at the moment the only reasonable thing to hold on to.

Mamma, her face more luminous than ever announced to us: Children, we are leaving for Rhodes!

I was little more than three years old and I did not know where Rhodes was, but Attico's eyes told me, reassured me, that we would be going there together.

The happiness and enthusiasm of my parents was tremendous. It infected us as well, so much so that we became impatient and hotheaded, difficult to control.

We left again from Brindisi, this time destination Rhodes. It was 1936 and my memories of it all are spotless.

The motor vessel was called the Rex[2]. It was magnificent. Majestic and white, it stood out against the sky. I looked at my brother, his face turned upwards and his eyes full of miraculous wonder mixed with a bit of fear. That ship was too enormous for our little eyes. I squeezed his hand in mine and looked at my parents, who were so calm and assured. My whole world was there with them. Then the ship seemed smaller to me.

We boarded and followed the usual routine, accounting for suitcases and cabin assignment. The discovery of all of this was, for us children, new and wonderful.

Everyone embarking on the ship came from various regions of Italy, each closed in their small family worlds, but all united in the expectations and the hopes they shared. They were also bonded by the shared heartache of leaving Italy, a heartache that over time would be transformed into a wrenching grief.

Every day during the crossing the Captain hosted at his table a different family. For our occasion I remember that my mother was extremely elegant, decked out in a blue dress with white polka dots, a rose pinned to her shoulder. But no flower could have ever competed with her beauty and her expression, shining with joy.

My father wore a dark suit and an expression severe enough to hide his concern that his hair would not stay in place, as it was meticulously groomed to cover his prematurely bald head.

I was rather absorbed by the task at hand, which was to go over in my mind all of the requirements my mother had given me: remain composed, don't chew with your mouth open, don't interrupt when the adults are speaking, and many other rules I don't remember anymore.

A waiter lifted me up and delicately set me down in the chair. My little organza dress floated at any little movement. I felt all grown up, beautiful, and important. I searched for the glance of Attico and his comforting reassurance, but his attention was completely focused on the table. He seemed to me intimidated by so many things - the number of utensils and glasses, the spotless uniform of the Captain, and the sparkle of his gold plated buttons.

Everything went very smoothly until the inevitable. The catastrophe.

The waiters came into the dining room wearing black pants and white jackets. Their arms were raised to hold up the trays upon which were enthroned big, fat roasted chickens with the drumsticks pointing up in the air. A splendid white flower was positioned on top of each.

The flower petals floated up and down at every step of the waiters. After my initial astonishment of this spectacle, I forgot in the blink of an eye all my mother's instructions and her threats of what would happen in the case of any possible tantrum.

I disregarded above all the severe look of my father. I disregarded even the light pressure of my mother's hand on my arm, and her threatening glance.

I wanted those flowers. I wanted them all. And I began crying and thrashing myself around.

Mamma slowly rose, took me by the hand, smiled at the captain, and despite my reluctance, my tears and my complaints, she accompanied me out of the dining room.

Our exit lasted only a few minutes but I remember it still very well.

When we re-entered, the captain rose. My mother, with some curls out of place and the rose on her shoulder a little displaced, excused herself for the unexpected exit, inviting everyone to continue the lunch from where it had left off.

At the center of the table stood a stunning bouquet of white flowers, but I didn't want them anymore. I felt only an aching burn on my backside, insistent, but even today I believe it was very much deserved.

We began to see Rhodes come into view and all of us went up on the bridge of the ship. I had arrived at the railing and I will never forget how my mouth brushed against it, leaving me with a taste of iron and salt water.

I can once again see the high walls which, like a treasure chest, protected the wonderful city of Rhodes. Tall and imposing, they surrounded all of the city's historic beauty.

I recall the amazement on my parents' faces and my mother's tears. I still feel my hand squeezed in that of my brother.

At three years old you don't know what eternity might be. But I felt it in the grasp of that little hand only slightly bigger than mine, and I heard it in the voice of the little boy who said to me, "Here Mimmi, we are home."

Home. And here begins in full force the odyssey of my wandering family.

We made a brief trip from the city of Rhodes to Cremastò, a little fishing village. Cremastò was chosen not because it was more pleasant, but solely for its greater proximity to Maritsa, the airport where my father was to work.

The house we found had a little courtyard closed in by walls that seemed to me incredibly high. Inside there was a huge room and in one corner a type of elevated platform bordered by a frail railing that in my opinion, at the time, was fantastic. A ladder with just a few rungs led directly up to it. The platform was what the islanders called "krevati," essentially a bed for the whole family.

For us the platform would serve as a storage area.

Everyone looked at Mamma, who was frowning but smiling...a good sign!

She said, 'We are all tired, tomorrow we will find something better!'

"Tomorrow" is a word that for years had a sinister sound to us. My father was an expert in words. At the sound of the word "tomorrow", he rested himself against the doorframe in a strategic position, ready for a possible escape. Mamma went closer to the krevati on her tiptoes to inspect and examine it. With delicacy she lifted the low mattress.

A strangled scream and an expression of disgust were immediately followed by a swarm of bedbugs that began to run off in all directions, transforming the krevati into a battlefield. The rebellion of the bedbugs was unanimous - those little offensive creatures, determined to bite and sting all over since they had been disturbed and vilified.

Papà with the suitcases in his hands quickly reached the front door. Mama said, "the children are tired, let's sleep in a hotel and tomorrow we will figure something out."

The tomorrows piled onto one another fast and furious.

LIFE IN CREMASTO ON THE ISLAND OF RHODES

The availability of houses was rather limited and we ended up staying in the one with the krevati and the bedbugs. My mother resigned herself to the presence of those annoying insects. They had arrived there before us and had settlers' rights.

But we didn't sleep on the krevati. We slept on traditional beds instead. As for the krevati, it served as our favorite game, and we were at peace with those stubborn insect residents.

The village of Cremastò was truly tiny, made up of a few houses and a piazza cobbled in mosaics. These mosaics had the tiniest stones of black and white. Arabesque decorations braided themselves together to form thousands of figures, figures so beautiful that the houses that faced the piazza seemed humble, further enhancing the splendor of the piazza.

An unpaved road led from the village to the sea. On either side of the road were crumbling shacks. Fences, more suggestions of fences than real ones, hosted every type of domestic animal. But the true kings of the land were the goats, there were so many goats.

And then, there was the sea.

Transparent waves skimmed the tiny bay, caressing stones of a thousand colors, shapes, and sizes, and transforming them into a myriad of precious gems. Every time a wave withdrew, it swept away its own transparency and radiance, only to bestow it again on each return. The stones were rocked back and forth by the incessant caress of the sea. An eternal game of illusion and dream.

The immensity of that huge mirror of water intimidated me. While its clarity at the shore was inviting, just a few meters away the turquoise crystal water turned into a deep and mysterious blue. I would look for the reassuring presence of my parents and all the fears for the unknown sea would suddenly disappear.

The time arrived for Attico to do his First Communion, and frenetic preparations kept my mother busy practically all day, every day. A constant help was guaranteed by her friend Ersilia Fontani, whose husband was Papà's colleague and best friend. Theirs was a true friendship, one which had faced time and distance, loyal and steadfast until the end.

I like to think about the four of them in heaven now, as they were in Cremasto, playing cards and laughing until they cried.

The Fontani family lived near us with their two daughters, Fiorella, who was my age, and Mirella, a little younger. I would be remiss in not mentioning them as a part of my childhood, for they represent a stable period in my vagabond life. Later on in our lives we found ourselves scattered far apart, but always we managed to find each other, strong in an absolute and ineradicable bond.

The night before Attico's big day came. I didn't really understand the importance of the event. But as I thought of my brother dressed properly in his first important suit, and of all the frenzied preparations and joyful atmosphere, I was euphorically happy.

Mamma was rolling the pasta dough with confident and expert motions while ungraspable little clouds of flour floated in the air. Her hands seemed to just barely brush the rolling pin and the dough would expand, assuming the form of a perfect sphere.

On top of strips of this luxurious dough were arranged portions of ricotta. Papà had gone to buy the ricotta at Pevaragno, a town a little farther away. There the dialects wove together in a civilized coexistence. Almost all the citizens there were originally from northern Italy, and effectively had transformed that town into a miniature Italy with its same crops and long rows of vineyards. Every time my father went there he would say to my mother: "Elvira, I'm going to Italy!"

Signora Fontani, tall and with hair as black as tar, was expert at closing the ravioli. She would press a fork on every side, sealing inside the fragrant stuffing. Then one by one she would line them up on the white tablecloth. This sequence was closely observed by eight astonished eyes, amazed by her prowess.

Suddenly, Papà burst into the kitchen like a cyclone, out of breath. With his tuft of hair blown by the wind, he relayed unexpected news. Abruptly the chain of ravioli production came to a halt, and one raviolo sat only half closed.

A decisive and absolute decree had been released. All of the First Communicants, both Italian and Greek, must wear the government issued patriotic school uniform. This uniform was called the 'uniform of the children of the wolf'. The wolf, of course, was a strong symbol of Rome and Italy since Etruscan and Roman times.

The adults were in total shock, while for us little ones, the bigger interest was towards the half closed raviolo.

Mamma rested a sad glance on the clothes hanger where Attico's suit hung: the double breasted jacket, the white dress shirt and the pants that were awaiting a final decision as to whether they would be held up with a belt or with suspenders.

Mamma diverted her gaze, trying to forget the cost and the numerous trips to Rhodes to source everything for the suit. Turning to Papà, she asked: 'Why?'

My father explained that if all the Italian children had worn their beautiful dress clothes, it would have created a cruel and useless discrimination against their Greek peers. For this reason the authorities had decided to render all the children equal, privileged or not, and the permitted dress would be the school uniform, which all children owned.

My mother smiled and set up to freshen the school uniform, but a new worry came across her face: Attico had lost his blue handkerchief, the fundamental accessory of the school uniform.

There wasn't time to go back to Rhodes to search for it, but suddenly and with a cry of joy, Mrs Fontani went to the kitchen window with a feline spring in her step and grasping the blue curtain pronounced: 'Here is your blue handkerchief!'

The First Communion of my brother went off swimmingly...and that day I remember as a marvelous day.

We were not to remain in Cremastò for much longer.

1938: THE TOWN OF TRIANDA ON RHODES

"When the evening fades
In the fountains, my hometown
Is a faint color.
I am far away,
I remember its frogs, the moon,
The sad quivering of the crickets..."

- P. Pasolini

We moved to a town called Trianda. It was between Cremastò and Rhodes, but closer to the latter.

Mamma, in her continual search for something better, managed to find a house in the country. I would say by today's definitions it was a villa, but back then it was not called a villa. It was a house.

It was 1938 and my mother was expecting a baby. Her body was a little heavy but her eyes more luminous than ever. And my brother and I were at the peak of a wild and still untainted happiness.

We had the large house all to ourselves, an enormous garden full of wonders to discover that surrounded the house, and a little baby on the way that we would soon be able to cuddle. The house was positioned near a fork of two roads. One was a paved road that led to Rhodes, and the other was a dirt road that led to the center of Trianda.

At the point where the two roads met there was a large green gate designated for the passage of cars. You could count on one hand how many cars had ever passed there.

At the left was a smaller gate which was always open, in fact the only gate open. From this gate, you winded up a road that went slightly uphill. Our house could be seen there, up above the fork in the road.

Halfway up, the road widened to make a larger space. Here a couple of benches were placed, one on the right and one on the left. They seemed to invite a rest, then once again the road continued and narrowed as you approached our house.

On either side of the road were olive trees hundreds of years old, their branches contorted to form thousands of shapes we found either harmonious or terrifying. The olive trees were interspersed with bushes that in spring were mantled in a myriad of perfumed blossoms.

The road finished in a little piazza, and there was our mother's terror and nightmare, a water well enthroned in the center of the piazza. Upon our arrival, it was closed almost immediately with a cover and robust padlock.

Three small steps led to a terrace ringed by an iron railing, and there was the main entrance to the house. Two doors and two iron door knobs.

I remember that the entrance was huge, but I was little. To the left was Attico's bedroom, to the right was the living room and straight ahead the bedroom of my parents, the dining room, kitchen, and small bathroom.

The floor was a white graniglia stone, and around the perimeter were more black arabesque designs of leaves interwoven with flowers.

The entrance was the coolest and airiest part of the house, and also the most crowded during the scorching days of summer.

Absolutely forbidden to us little ones was entrance into the living room. Access there was allowed only to privileged adults who could walk on the soft rugs and sit on a couch that seemed destined to have countless and perfectly beautiful pillows.

What a delightful transgression it was to leave the door ajar in order to peek at that which we were not allowed to touch. The table had delicate and tapered legs made up of fragile wooden spheres lathed to rise one on top of the other.

My celluloid doll with its sky blue romper rested on a chair, its gaze fixed and always the same, it's facial expression unchangeable. The doll represented the presence of children but without the possibility of damages to that room from any real children.

The dining room had a deep blue credenza and a long table, which we all gathered around together. Harmony and laughter hovered there, but also my jealousy of my brother. I could not understand why my mother would give him bigger portions at meals - it seemed to me discrimination, despite the logical explanations of Mamma.

The bedroom of my parents was large, with two windows that looked onto the garden. Next to one wall was a little bed for me, and then along a longer wall their big bed.

The walls were covered with tapestries, large and fluffy rugs that came from a maker in Trianda. The chest of drawers was spacious. In one corner sat the 'visavi', a type of dressing table, an important basic piece of furniture in every Greek bedroom.

I can almost still see Mamma looking at herself in the mirror, back when she was pregnant with my brother Franco. I would go up to her and put my face and my hands on her belly. Often I felt a light fluttering and I thought that inside there was a part of me, of my little world that was expanding but that would remain my world.

Those were marvelous years, characterized by harmonious co-existence between Italians and Greeks. There was reciprocal esteem and respect for the two languages, and for the two religions, Roman Catholic and Orthodox. Respect for the one and only, indissoluble God.

Naturally, the bond that grew among the Italians was even stronger, as we were united by nostalgia, memories, and love of our homeland Italy.

Today people talk about those years as full of hatred and suffering, subjugation, liberty denied, and ideology imposed. Nothing is more false, I was there!

I spoke a mixture of Italian and Greek, as I spent time with all the children without distinction. Children are the same everywhere in the world. They don't know hatred, and racism does not reside inside them. Children are cheerful and pure.

Adults, instead, often love to invent falsehoods and recount things that don't exist, until they even become convinced of their own manipulated truths, sullied and defamed.

On February 16 of 1939 my brother Franco was born, born at home, as was the custom in those days. Early that morning at our house a huge woman was introduced to us. She was big and tall with an immaculate apron, and she began issuing strict orders.

My mother's friend arrived too, at which point Attico and I were accompanied to the house of some Greek friends. My brother and I agreed between the two of us that, considering the atmosphere around us was charged with electricity, we would go along with this transfer without any questions.

We spent the whole day overwhelmed with a sort of anxiety and mystery mixed with curiosity. This created inside of us the sense of a real time bomb.

Finally that evening Papà came to pick us up. We caught sight of him on the horizon walking with a confident and victorious stride, his same lock of hair flopping in the wind.

The road home seemed to me endless, never had any stretch of road seemed as long.

We entered the room of my mother. Her hair was spread out on the pillow and her eyes seemed like shining stars, while she held to her chest a bundle of white wool.

Delicately she pulled away the blanket and a little rosy face under a shock of blonde hair fixed its black and penetrating gaze on me. I looked at Attico who had the same expression as me: dumbfounded wonder for such a miracle as this.

THE CITY OF RHODES

"I dreamed in my life dreams that
Remained forever with me,
And that changed my thoughts
They passed through time and through
Me, as wine through water,
And they changed the color of my mind"
- 	Emily Bronte

The time came for me to go to school.

My most vivid memories were the weekly excursions to Rhodes, an occurrence much anticipated by the adults, while we children both loved and hated it.

We put on our most elegant clothes. My father dressed in his military dress uniform. My mother exhorted Attico not to get too close to the gate with his good suit on. She called out to me to not kick at the rocks, reminding me that I was not a tomboy.

Franco, on the other hand, was held by Papà and was exonerated from any scolding because he was too little.

The first to board the bus was Mamma, then me, then Attico, and my father took up the rear with Franco in his arms.

The long paved road went past Trianda with its sparse fisher-man's houses. The huge dark sea flanked us on the left, made more elegant by the soft lace that every wave brought towards us before breaking on the shore.

On the right there was a stretch of road where the rocks seemed to brush close by to us. I was frightened by the sight of them and tried to slide down in my seat, but my curiosity propelled me to look up.

A mountain of massive boulders seemed like they might crash down at any moment. They were at the mercy of a very delicate balance, seeming more inclined to roll downhill than to remain in their precarious situation.

Agave plants were everywhere among the rocks. Papà explained to me that agave plants flowered only once every hundred years. They represented the only element of hope and firmness that I could see in that chaotic mass of rocks.

Finally on the horizon Rhodes appeared. This was a clear sign that the dangerous rocks were behind us. We were now free to discover beauty fused with harmony in a triumph of colors and fragrances. It is not my imagination but how it was.

On one side of the main piazza was the Hotel of the Roses. Cascades of lush flowers and branches were woven together to decorate the hotel facade and its arches, bestowing a flavor of a fairytale.

Little paths led away from the mandracchio[3], a small fishing harbour, towards the center of the town. Everywhere the famous roses of Rhodes reigned supreme.

We arrived at the wonderful harbor. Here they had erected a commemorative stele, or stone column, that supported a statue of a fawn[4]. Throughout the town there were also real fawns and deer that you could see frolicking around, beloved and protected by the whole town.

It was really the harbour that was my favorite thing to do. I sought out the fawns, and carefully I would try to get close to them. Their fur shone in the sun, and I tried to provoke their interest.
Once a fawn approached me, its gaze fixed on a bow that wove

through my hair. It played around with the bow, nibbling it with its mouth until it had loosened it. Then with a regal pace the fawn left.

My father would often tell us the legend of Rhodes and we loved to hear it.

A huge man had placed himself at the entrance of the harbor with a widespread stance. The ships, in order to dock on the pier, had to pass underneath him.

It was the famous and mythical Colossus of Rhodes[5].

For my tender years it was too difficult to understand the significance of such a presence. I found the leaps and acrobatics of the deer much more interesting.

Even more fun were our forays into the mandraki, the great market of Rhodes. Here you would encounter strange people. Women who peddled every sort of commodity. Men who sold the local specialty of sponges, which they hung all over their bodies, transforming themselves into clumsy monuments of foam.

The mandraki market was a confusion of shouts and exhortations to look and to buy, in every type of dialect and from heavily delineated visages. My mother's preferred goal was the perfume shop and Mirù, the young sales girl who had become a dear friend to us

Mamma would buy a face powder called Kaloderma, and the little box for me was a source of wonder. The cover was decorated with perfumed flowers and inside was a fluffy pink puff, perfumed and mysterious.

The undisputed lords of the market were the Jewish people, who were highly respected and admired by everyone.

We saw Mirù again later, after the war. She had just gotten back from a German prison and she stayed in our home for a few days. She was seeking out all the people who had demonstrated affection for her, and we were among those people. After she overcame her initial shyness, Mirù began to speak of the happy times in Rhodes. But she also spoke of something unthinkable and absurd when she was a victim in Germany. Long conversations with Mamma that don't have any validation in that which is said today.

She had a black bob haircut and copious bracelets adorned her wrist. One was a charm bracelet from which hung little rings and jingled many tiny little objects, among them a grinder, a star, and many others I don't remember.

At times I ask myself, how is it possible that all the Jews that were with us in Rhodes died? Is there anyone who feels the need to spend even a single word in favor of the Italians? Mirù had the courage to do so - are there any others?

Our time in Trianda was marked by an event that I remember very painfully. I broke my arm, which required me to stay in the hospital for about two months.

The hospital was in Rhodes, and it was a structure constructed by the Italians. I remember the long corridors and the spacious windows that ran along them. Outside was a green lawn that ran all the way to the sea, where the lawn seemed to remember it had to stop right there, for the sea was an insurmountable border.

My hospital room had two single beds. When I arrived, everything was agitated and I was incredibly disoriented. I covered my face so as not to see my body racked with pain and aches. I didn't want to turn and see my arm hanging loose or hear the stabbing cries of my mother. After a bit, I went into total silence, I just listened and half closed my eyes.

A young girl, little more than a baby, was drying her tears with the sheet and asked with a delicate voice my name and what had happened to me.

"Mimì", I said, looking at my arm, held together tightly with bandages and bags of sand. "My arm is broken. It was my father's bicycle. I wanted to get on it. I'm big now.'

She looked at me, then said, "I rested against the railing of my terrace and I fell."

She stopped crying and began to console me. Her sweetness calmed me and then she announced the arrival of my Mamma with a voice that filled me with peace: "Don't cry, Mimì, your mother is here!"

Often her father came to visit her. He was a man small in stature and always dressed in black. He would caress Giovanna's face and his hand would lightly lingered in her hair. He always stopped near my bedside to see how I was and to encourage my parents, trying to emanate to them a hope that perhaps he didn't have.

They were Jews and they loved their God.

Why is there this hatred now towards Italians of that era. Is it possible that these memories are only mine, that no one feels the necessity and honesty to rise up in our defense?

I will die with that extraordinary mirage, but I was there.

Everything continued as before. I would accompany Papà to the gate when he left for work. He would get up into the truck to head to Maritsa. Eventually I would head back to the house, and to pass the time, naturally would hit my head against the fence pole. I never gave up on this childish pastime! It was easy for me to convince my child's mind that the pole was moving, instead of my head, and it made my head stronger.

SCHOOL PERFORMANCE

At the time, I was going to the elementary school in Trianda. On the school's facade were two columns that seemed enormous. Up high was written 'Italian Elementary School' and inside was a large hall with many classrooms and many students without division of race. Everyone was propelled with respect and harmony towards the mystery of learning.

My first and forever unconquered disappointment was to be always too young to put on the older girl's uniform and participate in the first row of children raising the flag. It was a dream that was never realized. When I was finally big enough, the italian girl uniforms had already passed out of style.

On the inside of the school was a spacious theater and a stage. The Italian community was inspired to put on performances, and in this they were led by the scholastic director Macrelli. He was from Emilia Romagna, and a great organizer and leader. Both Greeks and Italians participated in dance performances and entertaining comedies. Everyone who participated was passionate and convinced of their parts. We were all delighted for these interludes. Our schoolwork suffered a bit from all the time we spent in preparations at the theater!

We girls were experts in knitting and crocheting, while the boys focused on sports like various jumps and also running. And so it went on, resulting in a rather picturesque panorama in which the Greek and the Italian melted together. There was a blending of approximate verbs, phrases barely spoken and for that all the more repeated among us, a precursor of secret codes.

It was almost Christmas and eternal spring in Greece reigned supreme in all its splendor.

A great play was being planned and all the preparations had begun. An initial meeting assigned the tasks and roles, and a huge organizational machine was set in motion.

Everyone participated in some way. Young sailors put together the sketches and comedies. The gorgeous Cyprian wife of one of the aeronautic officials bewitched everyone with her charm, which was enough to make the show right there.

The children made up the dance corp. My mother did not participate in the play as she was too occupied with Franco who was just a little over a year old. But Papà was given things to do and as usual was an actor covering the role of an old man, even though he was only forty.

A role was also worked out for me, a singing role. It was decided that the song should be 'Bring a big kiss to Firenze', a perfect choice as I was Tuscan. The pairing would have been a great and moving success.

In the rehearsals, however, with a tentative step and my heart pounding, I began the first verse. The experts who were there to decide my future as a singer were left speechless. At the peak of their horror, they determined it was terribly necessary to enact an immediate "request of independence" on behalf of Firenze.

After some frenetic discussions, it was decided that I would be moved to the children's dance corp. Their childlike and delicate movements as a group would captivate the attention of the audience, without drawing attention to any one individual.

My outfit was selected. A green suit that covered my whole little body and legs in the form of a green stalk. A sweater of the same color that gave the idea of leaf branches. And a luxurious rose, the petals of which framed my face.

I rehearsed some of the dance steps, putting forth all my concentration and effort possible. I tried not to smile so as to hide my two huge new incisor teeth that seemed to have been lent to me by a beaver.

I panted a little from the dance, and, under the attentive and impartial gaze of Mamma listened to the verdict. She pulled me onto her lap, smiling, said, 'Ninni, this time you will be in the audience, you can be in the play next time around.'

I never ascertained what might be a possible placement for me in the artistic world, but there was never another play in which to participate.

RHODES AND THE SHIP OF REFUGEE JEWS

Maybe I wasn't suited to the theater because I wasn't delicate enough. Or maybe because I preferred to emulate the endeavors of Tarzan. I adored being in Attico's company and I followed him in everything that was challenging and dangerous. Climbing trees, learning every branch, hanging until my hands burned, feeling the roughness of the bark, coexisting with the huge salamanders, stealing from them the split between two branches, challenging them for the rights of their territory. Their brilliant eyes fixated on us and their tail strikes told us of their absolute displeasure in our arrogant invasion.

For the Greeks the salamander is a sacred animal, respected and defended. One can't really say it is beautiful, though. It is a big lizard with its back spiny like tree bark, denied even the privilege of a dazzling color.

On Fascist Saturdays, Papà was free from work. He spent the day doing sports. He took the young men on long walks to inspire them with a sense of duty and discipline.

Today that type of work is remembered as youth training in favor of cruelty and war, imposed with force and extortion.

Papà got up very early, always at the same hour, and after breakfast he got dressed. Gray green knickerbocker pants, black boots so shiny that they would have outshone even the stars, and a black dress shirt. And then, wondrous to me, the black band that wound around Papà's waist. He held it firm with both hands on his side, while I held the other end of the long band. Then slowly, slowly, Papà turned, winding the band around himself until my hands reached the end of the band at his side.

I was at the pinnacle of pride - my Papà was so very handsome. With one last glance he put his fez hat on his head and he was off, a proud look in his eye. The sound of his rhythmed steps clicked on the pavement, and the silk fringe decorating the fez moved at his every step, brushing in front of his face.

Satisfaction and love swelled in my heart. I followed him with my eyes from the garden, as he left. I was protected by the metal fence that closed everything in, and he was a little black spot swallowed by the distance.

It was 1940 or thereabout. The dates to me are a torment that pile up in a jumble that is difficult to sort through.

One day Papà came home earlier than usual. He was very agitated, and closed himself in the bedroom with Mamma. After a few minutes they called us, believing that we were old enough to understand what was happening.

A ship full of refugee Jews had arrived just off the coast of Rhodes. In an odyssey longer than a month, they had been humiliated by the absolute refusal of a docking in any coastal country, countries whose fear was stronger than compassion for these poor human beings adrift at sea.

It was the "bloodthirsty" and "cruel" Mussolini who ordered that the port of Rhodes be opened to that ship.

All the families on the island rallied without any difference of religion or nationality. There still existed compassion and generosity without barriers, there still existed humanity.

Mamma began to prepare packages. She scraped together every

little object that could be useful. Everyone was doing everything they could with enthusiasm and self-sacrifice in order to collect blankets, clothing, and anything that might be a vital resource for the desperate refugees.

Mamma called me over, holding between her hands my little fluffy jacket of white angora wool. To touch it filled me with joy, and to wear it, even though I had gotten a little too big for it, made me feel exceedingly elegant.

I ripped it from my mother's hands. It was mine, and the well explained reasons that supported the most logical of justifications went in vain. My desperation, egoistic and infantile, surpassed any reasoning.

We headed into Rhodes, and this time it was not for a pleasurable excursion but to help people who were struggling merely to exist.

The city walls of Rhodes were the same treasure chest of wondrous beauty, the pride of civilizations past and future. But this time the walls became a refuge for hundreds of human beings who were at the extreme limit of what can be endured.

We saw men, women, and many children with emaciated faces and desperate expressions, malnourished bodies awash in threadbare rags, and the frantic question, "Why, why?"

I pulled my little jacket to my face, I breathed in for the last time its perfume of warmth and I delivered it into my mother's hands.

In the long thread of my life, studded with knots, some good, some bad, this is a memory brimming with compassion and heartbreak.

To give cancels out every suffering. To give with love wipes out any regret. I often asked myself who was the little girl who was warmed by the warmth of my jacket. If she is still alive, I pray that she can think of the Italians not with hatred but at least with respect.

THE WINDS OF WAR ARRIVE IN RHODES

On the surface, nothing really changed. The regular get-togethers of my father and his friends continued, led by an official who we nicknamed "Panciolini" or 'Little Belly', for his small stature and his roundness.

Panciolini tried in every way to impress on others his way of thinking, sustaining that the war would be finished very soon and that unfortunately we would lose. At this point the other men got riled up, they raised their voices, and my father remained steadfast in his convictions.

The war, in the meantime, ignored my father's convictions, and it raged high and low.

With time, some of our deeply rooted habits changed. There were fewer heated discussions under the light of the moon. In our house an underground bunker was installed, accessed via a trapdoor in the dining room. We children, in our innocence, found these changes absolutely fascinating.

We slept in that underground room. We would open the trap door, and jumping in, we rushed down the stairs between laughs and jokes, ignoring the gaze of Mamma who was always more sad and worried.

Perhaps the bombings would have spared the underground room, situated as it was below sea level.

War is atrocity, death, and blood. We children were protected by our parents. They spoke under their breath, and if there was a wounded person they prevented us from seeing him. Death was a word we barely knew. If a chick died, they told us it wasn't dead, just sleeping, and that it would wake up in a bit.

For the adults, death is the end of everything. Its arrival is so dreadful and painful that only a deep faith can assuage it.

We children continued to play. Attico polished little stones, and then built structures with them. He would change them around, and even destroy them if one little stone disrupted the harmony of the whole.

I dug holes in the yard and put delicate floral compositions inside them. Then I arranged above them a piece of glass, making it fit perfectly to the ground. I would then ecstatically admire my little masterpieces.

Papà had explained to me that flowers maintain their freshness only up until they have consumed all the air trapped in the place where they are kept. I hoped to triumph over science in this regard, or I simply believed in miracles.

Our evenings on the terrace occurred less frequently and were shorter. Always at sunset the enemy airplanes arrived, punctually, compact, and confident. Immediately we received the order to go back inside. Meanwhile the noise from the planes became deafening, the moonlight rendered the shooting planes luminous in their nosedives, and thousands and thousands of lights rose up at the same time, making all the landscape seem as if it were day and not night.

Hundreds of rockets flew over Mount Fileremo. The huge cross there seemed melancholy because of all the airplanes that with precision aimed for Maritsa airport below, carrying with them death and fear. It was all perfectly executed, without error.

We children innocently followed everything that was happening through the window panes. My parents were my world,

Papà's hand rested on my shoulder and I felt safe. I was still too little to perceive the faint tremor in his hand and veiled fear in his voice, when he would say, 'Children, enough for tonight, it's time for bed.'

The cross on the mountain, symbol of love, peace, and brotherhood, was under attack, the bombings continued.

How many young airmen lie buried in foreign lands?

The airport was reduced to a heap of rubble, even the central command building. Many young bodies were ripped apart, boys who had been proud to be Italians, proud to put on the white uniform.

Everything had become dangerous. But life and a semblance of calm continued course.

Our days, those of Attico and I, were enriched by a new game: hunting shrapnel. We would walk alongside a bush of prickly pears. The pears which hung there had been ripped apart in a white and trickling slop, and behold, there underneath were the pieces of shrapnel, shiny, with a jagged edge, beautiful, each one different from the other.

All of the shrapnel pieces were messengers of death, but for us children it was a competition to see who could find the most. Then we would run down towards the sea, all the way to the military positions hidden under the sand. Along long sheltered communication trenches, Attico and I walked normally, while the soldiers were constrained to move between one place and another on all fours. We would reach a little widening, and little slits in the wall permitted rays of sun to enter. There the machine guns pointed out towards the sea.

The soldiers spent their time taking apart and polishing the weapons. The wounded soldiers were kept in a little deconsecrated church where many cots were aligned along the peeling walls.

When my brother and I would arrive a shout of joy would greet us, we were a little part of their faraway homeland. How many of them had left behind little brothers and sisters like us?

On the first cot was a soldier with his hands behind his neck and his eyes lost in the distance. On the wall were photographs with the edges frayed, portraits and smiling visages, many out of focus. How many of those photos were caressed and kissed in a desperate search for some remembrance?

I got a little closer. Among all of the photos, the face of a young girl jumped out at me, a braid framing her face like a halo. I reached out my hand to touch it but the young soldier blocked me.

"I only have that one", he said, and I understood that among all the photos, this was his most precious one.

I retracted my hand and responded, "She's beautiful", and he smiled at me.

Life continued on. There were sumptuous parties at the Navy and Air Force Club where people danced and laughed while biting into fluffy pastries. Wine glasses in hand, they had a euphoric happiness, too euphoric to be real.

The children didn't really understand, being children. But I believe now even the grownups were refusing to comprehend what was happening.

Things began to collapse. And then Mamma, a little heavy but always astonishingly radiant, was expecting Brunella.

The certainties that we thought were absolute began to vacillate, and Papà would recount under his breath to Mamma tragic events that to him were inexplicable.

He told her about cans that instead of containing gas held water, and about the corrupt dance of moving airplanes around from one airport to another, trying to show off that there were many planes everywhere, strong, and unbeatable.

[When Italy allied with Germany, they did not have enough materials to have military supplies, machines, and aircraft everywhere, so they pretended they had enough by moving the aircraft around from one airport to another, so that it seemed that every air base had aircraft.]

Even so, there were many forgotten heroes who fought past every sacrifice, who loved their country more than their own lives.

Italo Balbo - who can forget him? He was an example of supreme sacrifice, a hero, a man, a legend.

Papà told us that when the airplanes crashed into the sea, the search would continue until dusk, at which time the order was given to stop searching.

But Italo Balbo refused to follow orders. With an act of rebellion he ignored the order to stop searching, fearlessly jumped into his little airplane and took off. He found the fallen aircraft, with just one wing remaining above the waves. But he saved the pilot.

So many heroes, now derided and forgotten, but at the time they were certainly heroes. Their Italy was great, proud and appreciative of its heroes. This was my country.

And then everything collapsed. We no longer had simple nostalgia and longing. Instead there arrived a desperation for our relatives far away and for all the people we knew, because no one was safe any more.

The patrols continued. My father was now more frequently away from home, and my mother was pained to think about the baby she was expecting in this very uncertain and nebulous time.

Mechanisms were put in place to protect the safety of my family. Two teachers from the elementary school started sleeping at our house to protect us in case of some attack by dissidents.

The cross, symbol of the bombings, was shot down. The enemy was notably sophisticated. It had sent down paratroopers who were protected and hidden by some local Greek people. Once on the ground they furtively set up extensive positions for destroying every target.

The island was swept from north to south in continuation but the paratroopers were never found.

The two teachers at our house, Zucchini and Veluso, intensified their protection of us. To be honest, they were entertaining, always inclined to lighten the tension. But I felt much more comforted by the thought that sooner or later Papà himself would return.

Now I understand, with the wisdom that comes with age, where the paratroopers found refuge and protection.

In front of our house, beyond the secondary road, a high wall demarcated a mysterious and impenetrable property.

The owner was a little man always dressed in black, and we rarely saw him. He used a cane and he instilled in us a reverent fear. He would arrive, sweeping along the tree lined road that from his house ended at a gate marking the end of his property.

If mama came to the window, he would lift his hat and give a hint of a little bow, and then he was off up toward his house.

One day, Attico and I were playing in the garden, and as usual he passed, saluted and smiled. But this time he invited us to cross over the threshold of his kingdom. Mamma gave a quick gesture of permission for us to go, and we went through the prophetic gate.

As we walked he asked about our health, our games, but our attention was completely focused on keeping our pace in step with his.

The closer we got to the house the more it seemed very large. He invited us to enter into a cool room that was a little shaded from the outside, and he smiled at us.

Along the wall, down low, was an accumulation of sand - yes - sand, and there he sunk his hand and dragged out the most beautiful cedro lemon that we had ever seen.

Signor Drachidi, this was his name, invited me to sink my hand into the sand, dry and cool, and my hand too found one of the cedro lemons. It was an incredible sensation of smoothness and perfume, air and sun.

I looked at Attico, whose expression mirrored my sensations. Signor Drachidi then accompanied us to the door, and we ran along the tree lined driveway, eager to tell Mamma about our marvelous bliss.

Now - why were two children, ignored for such a long time, invited to visit his house at that time? I think I know why, now. Our calm innocence could have been used as an alibi - everything was revealed, everything normal...but?[6]

Spring was in full bloom, the garden was overflowing with flowers, yellow daisies with long stems. I broke them open, inside they were tender and juicy. The garden seemed to be an enchanted place, a jubilation of colors and sounds, the chattering of the birds and myriads of butterflies fluttered from flower to flower.

It was the spring of 1942. Everything changed. It wasn't fun anymore to sleep in the underground room. Searching for shrapnel stopped being an amusing challenge once we became aware that the pieces of shrapnel, despite their brilliance, were porters of death.

Everything seemed cloaked in a coating of sadness. The flowers seemed to ask forgiveness for their undiminished splendor. The fear of tomorrow began to slither among all of the Italians, they lost the confidence in their convictions, their hopes. Morning was no longer the prelude to evening, and the evening didn't mean morning would come, the beginning of a new day.

Many families were repatriated to the homeland Italy, including the Fontani family with Fiorella and Mirella. They headed to the unoccupied city of Rome, and hope of salvation.

Everything seemed to be waiting for something, but what was it? Sadness and fear veiled my parents' faces, revealing an awareness and a trepidation that our happy little world was about to come to an end.

One peaceful event was the arrival of Brunella. We had all been certain that the baby would be a girl. It was September of 1942, and for Attico, Franco, and me came the same transfer to the neighbors, the same frown on Mamma's face, the same midwife with her brusque orders. The arrival was imminent.

Anxiety and happiness to see Brunella overwhelmed us. Her little round face and her little hand tightly wrapped around mine, a light touch that unleashed in me that absolute maternal sense that seized me my whole life.

She was there! The grasp of her little hands and the spark in her gray eyes knocked interest in anything else completely out of me. My dolls were meaningless, now they seemed too motionless and quiet.

In Brunella, I found everything that I needed. Even though she was so little, like a cyclone she wiped out my own free will. She was our commander, despot, and complete delight.

I buried my face in her neck, where her hair smelled of a nest. I lost myself in the clearness of her eyes and the whole world for me was there in her kingdom.

With Brunella we had a happy interlude, it seemed like everything was almost normal. Like the quiet after a feared storm. We never imagined that what would come next would be so tremendous and unexpected.

My parents had their usual secret conference, then the unanimous decision: it was our right to know.

My parents, up until that point, firmly agreed: they had refused every offer of repatriation to Italy. Anchored instead to another land that seemed theirs, they had chased every fear away, and they had nourished a hope, always more ephemeral, that the war would end.

They had believed in the good common sense of mankind. They had been reassured in the certainty of the great nation of Italy and of the unity of the Italian people. In a few words, they had believed in an impossible miracle.

They were now far from home without any more hope. They knew now that everything was lost. And they knew that even if Nations are great, men can be small.

I looked at Attico, who was for me the last hope. If only on his face I had been able to glimpse a glimmer of comfort. But instead I saw a worried expression and his rebellious wave of hair, and for the first time I perceived before my eyes a defenseless child. It was in that moment I grew up.

It was September 19. Brunella had just been born, and for days I wandered around the house. The living room was no longer off limits. I wanted to capture in my mind every object and every corner. Even my favorite doll looked at me with absolute indifference, wrapped in her blue jumpsuit. In one corner was the red sewing machine, the latest present from last Christmas.

At nine years old, the thought of the future didn't exist. The only thing that existed was today, because I was living it. Tomorrow was too far away. But you can imagine our total desperation. Tears covered my face. A thousand "why's?", each one without an answer.

DEPARTURE FROM RHODES

The days passed inexorably. Our embarkation was determined to be October 13, a cruel and merciless occurrence.

I remember clearly the details of that last day. Mamma was making the bed with great care and was urging us to finish our packing more quickly. In a way, it seemed to us like just another outing to Rhodes. We went outside slowly, Mamma holding Brunella to her chest. Three bundles had been placed near the well.

The bundles were our luggage, 13 kilos per person. Suitcases and anything similar were banned because they were too heavy.

One bundle was made of a yellow blanket, its shininess dazed us. The second bundle was made of a sheet, and the third of a cloth of cheerful colors absolutely out of place, for there was nothing cheerful about that day.

The knots of the bundles at their narrowest point let free a swath of fabric that moved at every breath of wind, with an absurd attempt to mitigate the tragic situation.

A little farther away I was trying to soak in every little detail. Attico was occupied with a little rock, giving light kicks to it with lowered eyes. Franco, seated on the lowest step, was already revealing his character: if you need to wait a long time, it's best to do it in comfort.

A little further behind was Mamma, clutching tightly to her chest Brunella, who I think was about 20 days old.

The fringe of the blanket curled around my sister, and as it moved it seemed to pronounce a melancholy poem of farewell. The voice of Mamma calling to Papà brought us back to reality: "'Quinzio, did you lock the door?"

Papà grabbed with his hands the big door handles and with his knee pushed the door closed.
"Yes, it is closed. But in any case, as you know, after a few days I will come back to this house."

The little girl with the happy carefree life remained anchored to that doorstep. My life until that moment was yesterday, the future was tomorrow, and between those two points I had knotted the thread of my life.

The same port of arrival, the same city walls of Rhodes. But nothing like before, no intrepid hope. Instead, a dark fear of the unknown.

We boarded the ship. My face leaned against the railing, the bitter smell of rusty iron smothered the perfume of the sea.

Tears ran slowly down Mamma's face, slowly she lifted her face towards the sky and sang a song, desperate and heartrending, "Addio Tripoli bel sol d'amore", "Farewell Tripoli beautiful sunshine of love."

Slowly the ship pulled away from the dock, no songs of mermaids and no shouts of festive joy. A silence, deafening in its desperation, enveloped everyone, grownups and children alike. The children pendulated between the novelty of the situation and simple fear.

The great ship that was crossing the Adriatic sea and would bring us home to Italy, an Italy that was desired, praised, and longed for.

A ship marked with an imposing red cross, full of desperate exiles. The cross should have protected us from enemy attacks.

In reality, the fear was that it would help the enemy to target us even more precisely.

We knew well that human compassion, in war, has rather limited confines.

We were all assembled in the ship's large hall. Training began to best deal with the possibility of torpedoing.

The grownups were able to go down to the cabins at prescribed hours and for only a few minutes, only to stock up on basic supplies and clothing. We all slept in the large rooms adjacent to the ship's bridge. An official gave us the first lesson on how to put on the life preserver in the least time possible, with an indecipherable expression he pronounced his words clearly, accompanying them with slow and measured gestures.

He picked up the life preserver, a series of little inflated cushions. There were two arm straps to put on, long bands that closed in front as if it were a little jacket.

The color was captivating, orange. And if anyone there deluded themselves to think that this training perhaps was just an extra and exaggerated precaution, they should *immediately* rethink that. Because the danger was real.

His calm and impersonal voice continued. 'You should always wear your life preserver and keep it tightly laced during the day. During the night it will be useful on the floor as a cushion, always with one arm through an arm strap."

"The speed with which you are able to put it on will determine your survival."

Then, without a smile, he fled almost in a rush towards the exit, not wanting to see the total desperation on so many faces, afraid of questions that he could not answer, incapable of offering the least bit of hope, and hiding the fact that, in reality, in the event of a torpedoing, it would be very difficult for anyone to survive.

We chose our corner of one of the large rooms near the bridge, and that was our home for several days and nights. Mamma sat on the ground and leaned up against a wall. Her life preserver was untied, for it was too difficult to open it to nurse Brunella.

Attico and I were nearby, trying to implement the recent lessons of the life preserver. We tried putting it on the ground and laying on top of it, one arm through the arm strap. Its contact was not reassuring but my imagination helped me to transform it into a fluffy mattress.

Papà assigned us various duties in case of torpedoing. Mamma was to focus on Brunella, to hold her as tightly as possible, to protect her...but how? Mamma always had a terror of water.

Papà was to focus on taking care of Franco, who perhaps was the only one who really understood. With his indifferent and detached air, Franco determined the uselessness of all the lessons. Thus for him, the life preserver became a little train that he dragged from one end of the great room to the other.

Attico, since he was older, was to take care of me, something he had done for our entire short lives with infinite love.

At first, the life preserver training was all theory. But the real applied use would come when suddenly, night or day, without any warning at all, the siren launched into its sinister and strident scream.

Soon we were called on deck for a simulation of that which could occur at any moment. Papà was 42 years old and served as the head of the convoy responsible for calm and order. The younger fathers had remained in Rhodes since the war was continuing.

Papà went back and forth many times the length of the bridge. The bulwark was there, and in the first row were the children. Behind them were the grownups, ready to spur themselves to dive into the dark and hostile sea if the cry came, 'Every man for himself!'

When the alarm finished, we returned back into the great hall.

And thus on the ship we began, without any choice in the matter, to participate in a thousand year old game of cat and mouse. We Italians played the part of the mouse.

The convoy of ships proceeded. In the middle was the big ship with us on board. Another ship was on our right and still another on our left, each full of military, a desperate and dreadful bastion in case the enemy were able to intercept us. The torpedo would hit the ship that flanked us, young lives sacrificed for the salvation of women and children.

This is war, merciless and incomprehensible.

A military cruiser zigzagged ahead of us scouring for roaming mines. Submarines crossed under us. We never saw them but we knew they were there, and that at the cost of their own lives they would have defended and saved us.

During the nights the ship's speed increased, and during the day it slowed notably in search of hiding places between the islands.

I remember the Captain well, every now and then you could see him pass along the bridge.

He was tall, with white hair, his gaze lost in the distance. His furrowed brow was lacerated by an assignment too great, far too great. To be not just father and grandfather, but simply a cold strategist in a game of slaughter.

He employed the most subtle ploys to deceive the impetuous, ferocious, and determined enemy. Changes to our route and sudden nighttime stops in the middle of the sea. A coordination of many moving parts. He demonstrated that the mind, guided by the heart, can do the impossible.

A thread of hope slowly began to reappear. Now they talked of a new docking place instead of the original port of arrival. They had learned that the enemy had likely discovered our original destination and would be there waiting for us. It was further decided that we would dock during the night, unknown to everyone, trusting that the darkness would protect our disembarkation.

The ship drew close to land as best it could. There the disembarkation began slowly. The figure of the captain in white could be seen clearly by the light of the moon. Drained of all his energy he rested against the parapet, and like that he bid us farewell. Papà was the last off the ship. He saluted the Captain. Perhaps he thanked him, and his face was covered in waves of tears.

DISEMBARKATION AND TRAIN TO ITALY

And so we disembarked from the ship in the dark of night. It was an emergency situation, for the place where we landed was impassable and unknown. A path winded through the fields. We dragged along our bundles with difficulty. Soldiers helped those who were having difficulty.

A long line of people filed through the unexplored path, and they were focused on not losing any package, not dropping any bundle. These bundles represented to us our only riches in the world. The rest of what we held was fear, as well as the hope we would find a train crossing the Balkans that could carry us to Italy.

Finally, a dark and mysterious shape appeared on the horizon. A train that seemed to me too long, too ugly, and too dirty. But after so much time on the ship, that thought was mitigated by a quiet relief in having my feet on firm land.

On the train we were assigned a little compartment, with its wooden benches made shiny from a lifetime of use. Up high were three very picturesque bundles of our belongings on beautiful display.

We sat down, trying to find the least uncomfortable position. The train moved with a deafening and annoying creaking sound, the sound of old iron held together more by ingrained habit than by a logical mechanism.

Attico and I earned the window seats, Mamma chose a seat in the angle formed by the bench and the little wall that divided our compartment from the hall. She kept Brunella in that corner, a strategic place to keep her from slipping to the side.

Brunella, unaware of what was happening, had everything that was necessary: the love of Mamma and her breast swollen with milk. Meanwhile Franco was intently studying the purpose of a screw that was sticking out of the seat. Once he certified that the seat was stable, he became confident that he could lie down there.

Papà, always with much to do, went up and down the length of the train continuously. Twice a day he presided over the distributions of the rations, for it was his responsibility that everything proceeded in the best way possible.

Two young German soldiers carried a huge steaming pot of soup. They walked carefully sideways because the corridor was very narrow. They stopped in front of every compartment, rested the pot, and Papà with a big ladle filled the mess tins with a soup that smelled delicious and was miraculously hot. They continued until they had finished the length of the train. Then Papà stopped by our compartment and made sure we had everything we needed.

Above us, anchored to machine guns on the roof of the train, young German soldiers kept vigil for our safety. Perhaps they too dreamed of their faraway country, and the warmth of home. Exposed as they were to every bad turn of weather, they protected us from any possible enemy attack.

They came down at the change of shifts, about every two hours. They would pull tight their coats trying to warm up, pale, and emaciated. They looked at us dumbfounded. It was difficult to communicate with them.

How many of them returned to their homes? How many of them lie in Italian soil, betrayed, vilified, and martyred by the same people that they were protecting?

We were crossing the Balkans. We had left behind Greece, the land of eternal spring. Here instead it was winter, without any protection for we were inescapably dressed in lightweight clothing.

Striving for the least bit of warmth, we pressed together, one against the other.

We slept on the wooden bench, and the merciless cold infiltrated our nightmares. Papà was always the last to arrive. He had to constantly check that everything was in order on the train, going up and down the length of the train many times a day.

He lay himself out between Attico and me. He was frozen from the cold and we felt him shaking. All curled up, he tried as much as possible not to steal from us the little bit of warmth there was. We were too little to understand that even a father has some human limitations.

I would like to go back now, squeeze those frozen hands, smooth the worry lines from his face. You were only 42 years old! Thank you, Papà, for the values you taught us, for the inner beauty that you gave us to experience, thank you for the privilege to have had you in my life!

The train slowed in its pace and then stopped. There was too much snow and they had to free remove it from the tracks to proceed. Our desire to dive off into that inviting white sea triumphed over the exhortations of the grownups, and we got down from the train. The joy of the initial impact! Then the disillusion. Beauty doesn't always gratify its expectations.

A thousand needles began to torment my fingers, then a piercing cold gripped my legs. I had to make sure that my feet were still there, and with great speed I retreated to the relative warmth of the train.

With our faces pressed against the window, we watched what Papà was doing outside. He carefully washed the mess tins and slowly got back on the train. The tins clinked one against the other, giving off a sound that to me was almost pleasant.

The snowflakes fell slowly on the window and formed a myriad of dances, each one different from the other. They left behind a trail, drops which slowly streaked the glass.

The train started moving again on its way. But shortly after there was another forceful stop, this time not intentional and sudden. The wheels shrieked on the tracks, releasing a multitude of sparks.

Mamma was jolted, and shrieked. Papà and some soldiers got down from the train. Near the train's engine a small man, completely bundled up, was waving his arms in an agitated way, his hands raised in frenetic gesticulations. Only foreign words broke the silence, then finally with one eloquent motion, he indicated what was behind him.

Just past his shoulder lay a bridge half in ruins. His agitation suddenly had meaning. He had saved our lives, for death was just a few steps away. I saw my father get closer, perhaps to thank him. He shook the hand of the unknown hero, propelled only by human compassion. The man disappeared into the fog but left in all of us an indelible lesson.

After a few hours the train once again departed. The countryside was populated with little towns. Occasionally the train would stop for short periods and various soldiers would get on board.

There were also women soldiers, which was rather unusual for those times. They asked us about our needs, about our health, and gave us fruit, bread, and other basic necessities. When they asked Mamma if she needed anything else, she responded, "La speranza e le pezze per tenere pulita la bambina", which means, "I need some hope, and also some rags to keep the baby clean."

The nursing auxiliaries, now I know what they were called, brought Mamma some packages with fluffy Melton cloths. I was amazed that these cloths weren't white but instead big squares of gray and blue. This floored me, but I understood that the usage was more important than the appearance.

After a long journey we arrived in Postumia near Trieste, today a part of Slovenia called Postojna. After an orderly disembarkation from the train, we were grouped together in a large building and divided by Regions: the Tuscans, the Venetians, and so it went. Then by gender, the women were separated to one side and the men to another.

Shock and fear assailed me. I looked desperately for Attico and his protective reassurance. He was small and defenseless among so many men. Diligently there in line, he had the same fears as I did.

The first operation was to wet our hair with a sticky and malodorous liquid. My hair brushed against my face, it was uncomfortable and disgusting. Then once again we were lined up and headed to the showers.

The pleasure of hot water that ran over my body lessened my worries about being alone. Immediately after came the medical visit, the doctor kneeled down in front of me with a peaceful face and with a reassuring smile asked, "What is your name?"

I looked at him, and my nickname Ninni seemed to me absolutely out of place.

"Piera", I responded. "Piera, born 1933".

Silent celestial figures crossed back and forth across the room, a red cross adorning their white clothes. Then we were divided again by Region and finally my family was back together in their natural order.

1942: VENICE AND RE-ENTRY INTO TUSCANY

It was determined that the Tuscans would be sent first to the Veneto on their way home to Tuscany. The trip was short and we probably seemed like people on a pleasure excursion. Our bundles were taken and loaded on military vehicles to be delivered at our established destination: Venice.

We arrived at dusk. The lagoon seemed to me ugly and inhospitable, and I immediately lowered my expectations as the mirage of the luminous and perfumed island of Rhodes lacerated my heart.

A strange boat approached the pier. It was a gondola.

We got on board not without difficulty. Attico and I were interested in the new adventure, but Mamma refused categorically to get in the gondola, "Enough of the sea! I will go on foot!," she proclaimed.

The gondolier watched this scene, amused. Venice was a city of water, but Mamma had never been.

Babbo used every persuasive tactic he could think of, and finally Mamma got in.

The gondola glided sweetly between the narrow canals that wound through the tall palazzos, palazzos that seemed almost afraid to break the harmony of such beauty.

So many bridges! The gondola slipped underneath them and I

cowered into myself because they seemed too low. Finally the strange boat pulled up to a palazzo full of light. A soldier and an official were expecting us. They came down the three steps toward the water. The official extended his hand to Mamma. Taking her arm, he led her inside the marvelous palazzo, while we followed behind.

It was the renowned and prestigious Hotel Danieli. A spacious entry hall and plush rugs cushioned our steps. Smiling faces and handshakes greeted us, offering congratulations for our reentry into the homeland, and words of pride for the courage we had demonstrated.

I looked at my parents smiling as they sought normality where none existed. With no hope for the future, they enjoyed that moment as the only certainty that they had. As we entered the dining room, I forgot that my dress was too big and my shoes already too small.

My world was finally being put back together, and for the first time Rhodes seemed to me faraway. The dining room of the hotel was decorated with round tables adorned with tablecloths that went all the way to the ground. A small table lamp on each table gave off curious games of light and shadows. Each lamp's weak light emanated the halo of an uncertain situation.

Glasses sparkled and their transparency seemed to give off joyful poetry. We sat down together, understanding the sacredness of the moment. Then, between dream and illusion, Mamma's voice lacerated the silence.

"Quinzio, tomorrow what will we do?"

For me, that question even today announces a Tomorrow that never existed. It was a question that rang with a cruel and perfidious significance. It is a word should offer hopefulness, but in for me always poisoned and rendered bitter the Today.

We took off again on our voyage, this time heading to Orbetello, the town of my birth. We were going to the house of my grandparents, whom I practically didn't know. They had been yearned for and beloved, but never seen.

There, for the first time in my life I tasted a flavor of jealousy beyond any logic. My grandparents' house was the undisputed kingdom of my cousin Cosetta. She was the daughter of my uncle Argo, who was my father's brother. She was littler than me, little and rebellious, spoiled to the point of disbelief.

Given how close she lived to my grandparents and the other aunts and uncles, she had earned a monopoly of their affection and attention, which she had obtained by any means necessary. In her presence every demonstration of affection was sugar coated.

Sparking her jealousy was effortless and exceedingly perilous. She threw crying fits followed by a raging of reactions as unpredictable as they were dangerous. And with every little clash, I was growing up. I had to understand, I had to give in, and in such a way I habituated myself to being little or grownup on the basis of the needs of the moment.

As it turned out, I was also sick. I spent many days in bed, for the cold and suffering of the voyage had gifted me with bronchial pneumonia. Worn out from fever, I was set up in the big bed of my parents, and there I savored all the affection of my grandparents and aunts.. My colossal grandfather, certainly not in size but in heart, in knowledge and in understanding. And Aunt Vanda, the light touch of her hands, the furtive kiss on my hair.

As soon as I got better, Papà left.

Mamma told us, "Papà is going home, and soon we will join him."

And so we lived there, and the time came when we had to go to school. The school was a large edifice in the main piazza of Orbetello, which you reached by climbing a staircase. I held my school bag tightly under my arm, while the security of my grandfather's hand grasped mine.

My grandfather was the Scholastic Director of that school, but he left me alone on the doorstep of the classroom. All attention had turned on me, faces that were curious, winking, and hostile. The teacher was there awaiting the new arrival, and she triggered in me the same feeling as did the large chalkboard and the grandiose teacher's desk.

"You are tall," she proclaimed, "Last row."

Being tall seemed to me for the first time more a fault than a natural fact, which was a completely foreign concept to me.

The teacher approached me. I searched her face for a glimmer of a smile, but her air was severe and her expression rather exasperated. She overwhelmed me with a rapid fire series of questions.

"How old are you? What's your name? Where and when were you born?"

With a stentorian voice, mentally calculating my answers, I tried to respond.

"Orbetello - yes, Orbetello was my hometown."

I had in my response a solemnity and a pride that I didn't feel but which I hoped would earn me the possibility of not being a foreigner in my own town.

Incredulous and perplexed shrieks burst out, this could not be true, the little girls of the class all knew each other, they had attended the same school, they had never seen me, I didn't speak like they did.

And a doubt rose up inside me - perhaps my hometown was Rhodes and my parents had forgotten this? I have to admit that my Italian was rather picturesque. I interposed Greek words with Italian ones, and this inspired in them first awe and then collective and unstoppable hilarious laughter. Meanwhile I felt frustration and total estrangement from my town of birth.

Promptly the teacher tried to settle down the wild spirits, she took my defense, and she attempted to explain that I came from a faraway place. Then with questions always more insistent she took part in the entertainment.

At every mistaken verb, a hurricane of laughter erupted. Over time students and teacher got used to my apathy, to my gaze lost in the distance, and unanimously they diagnosed my absolute insanity.

When exiting, students would line up in twos, and beyond being tall I also became an odd unpaired number.

My impassivity floored them, and so they put into play another entertainment. They would wait for me at the exit for their assault. Then they ripped my school bag away from me, and when I tried to get it back they kept me away with pushes and kicks, everything with satanic pleasure.

When I got home I tried to hide my mussed hair, but concealing the scratches and bruises was much more difficult. Mamma attributed it all to my exuberance, she explained to me that the games with Attico were exaggerated and that I was a girl and not a tomboy.

But when my appearance when coming home from school did not improve, Mamma started to suspect something and spoke with Grandfather. At the exit at the end of school the next day, and in the midst of their mischief, my grandfather suddenly appeared. In the general fleeing chaos of all the children he took me by the hand and went up the stairs two at a time. Small and rather round though he was, to me he was transformed into a huge avenger. He entered the classroom where the teacher was meticulously organizing her desk.

She turned in terror at the unusual disturbance, her face waxy and her hands in a frenetic movement. She jumped at the fists that hit her desk. I looked at the face of my grandfather, his blue eyes, so sweet that they flared like flames, his eyeglasses having slipped almost to the point of his nose.

"Signorina," he thundered to the teacher, "There are no words sufficient to tell you what I think of you. Teaching is a mission, and goodness is a gift. You have neither one nor the other. I will see to it that you undertake the right path. You have amply demonstrated in your behavior that your vocation is neither teaching nor compassion."

He rested his hand on my hair in a light caress and said, "Why didn't you tell me?" My heart brimmed with love and pride.

Slowly my Italian got better. I reconciled myself with the school, and I continued by choice to be the odd one alone in the line. From that day I learned that there exist people that you love and others that you ignore. I never again let my goodness and manners be misinterpreted for weakness. I learned to defend myself on my own. And I also learned that life is full of little people who need to strike the weakest ones to show their strength. I learned that wickedness has no limits or boundaries.

Sparking pain is the first step for them, and if you demonstrate that you have fear then you are destined to become a victim. At every action you must be ready for the appropriate reaction.

My grandparents' house eventually became too crowded, and we found a little house on the Corso of Orbetello. We all slept in one room: Mamma, Brunella, Franco and I in the big bed. Attico slept in the big bed too but with his legs and part of his body on a type of extension made from an old trunk.

In the mornings we went to school, and in the afternoons we got to know and take possession of our town, and in particular our favorite place, the seaside.

We would go down a narrow street practically suspended between the open sea and the pond of Orbetello, it seemed like a long bridge - you can see it still today. There at the end was Santo Stefano, with a little railway for the local train, the tracks almost brushing the waves on the Orbetello side. Innumerable boats of all sizes would wait there to go out fishing. In the afternoons they were all there, anchored in place as best they could.

There on the seaside we had some of our most beautiful sensations and discoveries. The boats proliferated with tiny transparent crabs in continuous movement, they were called 'femminette' and with their eggs you could make a delicious pasta sauce.

I rested against a boat and followed with curiosity the crabs' extraordinary acrobatics as they arrived at the boat's edge and jumped into the sea. The attempts of the little crabs were repeated incessantly. So few achieved the dream of freedom. Many almost tasted the yearned for goal, then tumbled back into the bottom of the boat in discombobulated and desperate positions.

Santo Stefano with its castled houses and its position on the sea made us think of our recent times in Rhodes, ever present in our minds. Little by little Rhodes would become more distant, but it was always inside of us, indelible and vivid.

Too often the scream of bomb sirens sliced through the air. There was a general flight, everyone running towards the closest shelter. I remember the fear of not making it in time, the beating of my heart was astounding. Then the shelter and the desperate hope that Mamma was already there. And there she was...we felt saved, protected, and lucky.

In the shelter we would feel a reverberation, hardly perceptible at first, that would gradually grow closer. We recognized the sound of the bomber jets. They would fly in picturesque formation, a flock of silver dots in the form of a triangle. The jets shined like a thousand sparks of silver. Then pointing down in a precise nosedive, they unloaded clusters of bombs. Then the rumble of the motors softened, and the messengers of death soared back up towards the sky, while lacerating explosions mutilated the false silence.

With hearts in tumult we awaited the all clear. But it wasn't over.

A deafening roar announced a fireball in a frenetic dive, followed by machine gun fire along the roads. It was a scrupulous follow up to finish off what little had remained.

The projectiles struck the soil, and every strike gave off a little cloud. The jets would head back towards the majestic silver sky. On land remained those who weren't fast enough, laying in haphazard positions, the soil soaked with blood.

Then the all clear. Everyone went back home and life continued.

I often went to visit my grandparents house. My favorite thing was to be with Aunt Vanda, with the sweetness of her caresses and her empathy, she always managed to understand that veil of melancholy that would suddenly seep through me.

Grandmother instilled in me a certain awe. She was tall and willowy, always very busy, and had a marvelous braid that went around her face. Her ultra long hair inspired my wonder, long and voluminous. I would have liked to touch it, to stroke that silky black cascade, but my apprehension put a brake on this wish.

Grandfather, on the other hand, was small in stature with two incredible azure eyes that illuminated his face. He was determined, strong and decisive, and from him emanated a notable inclination for leadership and discipline. Confident of his ideals and principles, he kept faith in them even when Italy was no longer his Italy, when tragedy overwhelmed him.

I would go into his study on tiptoe, where he used to round out his salary by giving private lessons. There an imposing desk dominated the knowledge that floated in the air.

A leather armchair was there, imprinted with indications of his constant presence. Behind his shoulders lay a huge fireplace in dark stone. Instituted on the mantle rested the bust of Benito Mussolini, his penetrating gaze and a haughty scowl to be sure, which elicited in me respect and not fear.

On the walls were many paintings. One depicted Garibaldi, proud on his white horse. Another featured Mazzini. Others were of the many people who had contributed to the transformation of the Italians into one people.

On the walls straight ahead was an imposing crucifix, testimony of the greatness of our Lord and a reminder to us that He is great and we are fragile and small.

The days went on. The bombings had become daily and ferocious. The enemy had determined that the Via Emilia near Orbetello needed to be destroyed.

Attico's and my recklessness and the absence of even a minimum level of safety wore down Mamma's strength.

Word from Papà was ever more sporadic. We had gotten older, but not enough to understand the cruelty of war. Our outings in the streets of Orbetello represented for us the avoidance of a hostile world, but for Mamma were a source of despair.

Often the wailing of the sirens caught us far from home. Running, we reached the closest possible shelter, which wasn't always the same one as where Mamma had sought refuge. When the alarm came to a stop and we were able to find one another again, her face would light up with joy, incredulous that we were alive. Liberating tears fell in streaks down her face, revealing her anguish.

To us, honestly, her reaction seemed excessive. But out of the love I harbored for her, I resigned myself to the fact that I would need to be a little more domesticated and a little less wild.

Every now and then to keep me from running off, Aunt Vanda brought me to the office with her. She worked in the town hall, where she had her own desk and on it many white sheets of paper and colored pencils. I dedicated myself to sketching.

How wonderful, I could populate my mind with flowers and animals. But despite the fantasy and imagination, my mind wasn't able to be in line with my hand. Even with many tries and stubbornness, the dissonance remained absolutely unmitigated. I would imagine a flower or an animal but the result was continually depressing.

Aunt Vanda put an end to my art. The sheets were there, white and inviting. I tried to fill them with my unsteady handwriting. I recounted my voyage. My impressions took form and the sheets filled instead with writing.

Aunt Vanda read them meticulously. Every now and then she looked at me between the things that pleased her and things she didn't know about. She placed the sheets down, numbering them. Her red pencil marks with edits were much more numerous than the words, and I tried to convince myself that all that red was refining the writing like poppies in the field.

DEPARTURE FOR BERTINORO IN EMILIA ROMAGNA

I may have mentioned that during the last part of our stay in Rhodes, the elementary school teachers came to sleep at our house to protect us from bands of rebels. They represented a protection for us in the absence of Papà who was searching for the enemy paratroopers.

They didn't have families of their own to take care of and I remember well their names:

Zucchini, tall and reedy, taught me to ride bikes. Velluso, portly but crazy for all that was activity and sport.

There was also Macrelli, Scholastic Director of the Trianda school which I attended in Greece. I've lost in time my memory of his appearance, but their lives continue to fill my memories.

Macrelli came from Bertinoro, province of Forlì in Emilia Romagna. He was exuberant and unpredictable, and fulfilled to perfection the classic Emilia Romagna stereotype.

In Bertinoro he owned various properties, and in the crucial moments of our last days in Rhodes, he spoke to us about his opulent region. He proposed to my parents that in case of need, when we got back to Italy we could contact his sister who would take us in and protect us.

Mamma decided that indeed the crucial moment had arrived,

considering how dangerous Tuscany had become. She contacted Macrelli's sister, and with a proud gaze she became once again the marvelous pioneer that she had always been.

She expressed her justifications to my grandparents, and she had in exchange their openness and total comprehension. We children were entrusted temporarily to our grandparents. She alone, hopeful, armed with courage and determination, holding Brunella tightly to her chest, set off to conquer even Bertinoro.

She embarked on a solo journey full of adventure to say the least, characterized by alarms and unexpected bombings, rushed train disembarkations and forced stays in the company of strangers. She was often huddled behind an escarpment waiting for a train to resume its course. Finally she arrived in Forlì.

From there she took a motorcoach to reach Bertinoro, where she met Director Macrelli's sister Lina, who my mother described as a volcano of understanding and goodness.

And Mamma found a house for us. I would declare this a miracle, as the little town had already been overwhelmed by many refugees. Bombings in that area had been sporadic unlike the constant barrage in Tuscany.

It was different from other places where the tactic of the enemy was psychologically perfect: to destroy any human resistance with machine gun fire, bombings, and various oppressions. And for what purpose? In order to seize what? Mountains of rubble and desolation?

Now the massacre was concentrated on Tuscany, along the Aurelian Way, along the railroad. The targets were always the same, tedious. Wagons that flew into the air, tracts of roads stripped away, houses razed to the ground. Everything tiresome and already seen.

And so there in Tuscany, in a solitary "heroic" endeavor, a "bold" young man decided he wanted to liven everything up.

In the early afternoon he identified a peaceful place and had fun on his own. Just to feel heroic and invincible, he swooped in an inexorable dive towards the target of a merry-go-round.

Here unaware children were sitting on the little seats, grasping them with their hands. They rose up and down, carefree and happy to savor the inebriation of flight, cheering the air with festive cries.

Then the crackle of machine gun fire: murderous, precise, and relentless.

A profound silence, then desperate screams. Meanwhile the carousel continued its course, the little seats no longer anchored little hands clinging to gold poles, but scraps of living flesh, little angels without wings.

The merry-go-around kept turning round and round in a now useless lullaby. The only thing left was blood and the desperation of those who remained.

Mamma, terrorized by this episode, came back earlier than planned to Orbetello. She decided for an immediate departure to our new home. Our euphoria was extinguished in the sadness of leaving behind our grandparents and Aunt Vanda, and her tender and desperate embrace.

I would never see her again. During the civil war, she was loaded together with my grandfather in a wagon, exhibited as a trophy of war, insulted, beaten and humiliated. And only because she was guilty of respecting ideals that had guided her life and that of her father.

We left at dusk. Traveling during the night gave us greater security. We would need to arrive in Forlì early in the morning. We passed the night without sleeping. The darkness, the slow pace of the train, and the strange countryside - gloomy and mysterious - increased our anxiety and made us restless.

Attico had a precise assignment: he was named treasurer and was responsible for all the packages small and large as well as the suitcases. Those things represented our treasure and our future survival depended upon them.

They contained sweaters knitted by grandmother and Aunt Vanda in record time, blankets, and heavy clothing to face our second winter in Italy.

Attico took his new responsibility very seriously. I can see him now lightly engrossed in measuring and watching the net that was above the seats. There was a large package and a little one, then the suitcase, and then the smallest bundles nestled in the empty spaces between, all meticulously aligned.

He counted them, worried and on guard, one… two… three… then turning to Mamma said, "Don't worry, they are all here." He sat himself in the spot best suited to not lose sight of them, they were a precious treasure that was his to safeguard.

Attico seemed to be a little man with short pants and a jacket that had forgotten to grow with him. I looked at him. He had a delicate nose outlined with little freckles that sprinkled his face. Also he, like Papà, had a rebellious lock of hair. His incisors were slightly crooked and his dark eyes reported all his unease. The serene countenance of a child no longer existed and in its place instead was the distress of needing to become a man, without any choice in the matter, before it was time.

Little by little the first light of dawn illuminated the Emilia Romagna countryside. It was full of houses and long rows of trees that seemed suspended in lines, one tree after the other. There were many cherry trees and also mulberry trees. It was a marvelous countryside overflowing with human mastery over nature and divine natural wealth.

1943: ARRIVAL BERTINORO

The train, clattering and puffing, finally stopped at Forlì and we got off. I held Franco by the hand. He was indifferent, holding a piece of bread, nibbling it slowly. He savored the familiar taste amid all the agitated confusion. For him the only sure thing was the taste of that bread and there he focused all his attention.

We did a final baggage count, everything was there. The train station was a festive atmosphere of welcomes, kisses, and packages on shoulders. We made our way through a mix of people who were arriving and those who were waiting, and plunged ourselves towards the conquest of Bertinoro, a cheerful hilltop town.

We boarded a motorcoach that whisked us down the Via Emilia. Every so often little clusters of houses could be glimpsed, like Ronco and Forlimpopoli. Those towns later became tragically known for their only crime, that they existed too close to the most important Italian arterial road which united all of the peninsula, and which then of course had to be destroyed.

Above us we could see Bertinoro. The little town sat on the only hill for miles around and was thus the guardian of a great plain that led all the way to the Adriatic sea. From down below it seemed a pleasant and evocative fortress town.

The motorcoach, once past the little village of Forlimpopoli, scrambled up for the climb that carried you to Bertinoro town. We passed a little hamlet made up of farmhouses called La Bisciara. There, rows of vineyards stretched out and outside the houses laundry was drying, blowing in the wind like flags, a taste of peace already forgotten.

The climb up became steeper, the hobbling along of the old motorcoach became constant. And suddenly we had arrived in the piazza. It was surrounded tightly by houses almost as if to protect itself. A little wall separated the piazza from the road beneath, and it teemed with people, those seated and those on foot, without limit of age or gender.

Everyone was in an agitated state of waiting, curious eyes were everywhere, people who had fled towns no longer safe or liveable, all of them refugees like us.

We got off cautiously, aware of our rather unusual appearance, and among so many investigative eyes we looked for a friendly face. Before we could find one, however, and before we could slip into disappointment, an amazing thing happened.

An avalanche overwhelmed us, an avalanche of kisses and hugs and then the delightful feeling of finally being home.

Lina Macrelli was not only a volcano of generosity but a paean to brotherhood and solidarity. She seized Brunella and led us toward home, Attico frowning because he had lost control of the bags.

The narrow street closed in by rather tall houses winded slowly uphill. All the people who hadn't found a spot on the wall followed us: an embryonic ragtag army.

We came to a second piazza, and this one featured the cathedral and town hall, massive and imposing. Directly ahead of us, its noteworthy arches delineated and emphasized the importance of that seat of power. At the top of the roof the battlements stood out, perhaps to refine everything, last minute decisions of the designer. We children asked ourselves if it was an imposing palace or a castle?

In front of the town hall running along the length of the piazza, was an overlook, or Belvedere. Here your gaze became lost down over the city and further beyond various towns small and large. And a little further on, in the distance, was the azure of the sea.

We climbed higher from the piazza. Mamma was panting as she tried to harmonize her step with that of Signora Lina. Just before we reached our new home there was a large sad building on the right with windows and railings. It was the Seminary, positioned just at the corner of the Church.

The clergy had a prominent importance in Bertinoro. There in the highest part of the Seminary, there where it seemed like a castle, there lived the Bishop.

Finally we stopped. Ahead of us were two little steps and a small front door. We went in in single file, Mamma first and we followed behind. I held my breath, and my heart was in tumult as we savored the sacredness of the moment. We went into the living room. In the center was a table, and in a corner was an imposing terracotta oven and a red armchair.

Mamma approached the chair and said, 'Signorina Paolina, we have arrived.'

From the armchair a miniscule figure dressed in black stretched out a hand, so diaphanous that it seemed transparent. She turned towards us, and we saw that a light pallor veiled her face. A long cascade of white reached beyond her waist like beautiful cornsilk. For me she personified the symbol of a magical fairy.

Slowly she rose towards the garden. With her hair she tried to hide a protuberance on her back. I looked at Attico and saw on his face a calm indifference. For us she was the Signora Paolina, it did not matter if she had a hump on her back.

She turned towards us, and on her face was a dread of what our reaction might be. How many times had she had to confront negative reactions, and how many more times would she need to do so? It was dread concealed by constant provocation.

I drew close to her and rested my face on her chest. I heard a riot of disordered heartbeats, but my gesture brightened her face and her fear of our reactions disappeared.

Slowly she stroked my hair. For me she was always the magical fairy. Her attentions to us, and the unconditional love she gave to Brunella, revived in her what she was never actually able to be - healthy, beautiful and full of life.

Sweet and silent, she had gone through life on tiptoes, and she died that way too. Perhaps God who had penalized her in life wanted to spare her all the atrocious occurrences that we lived through later on. Occurrences which transformed lovely Bertinoro into a place that made up a part of the famous and sadly known 'Red Triangle', characterized by days of calm more illusory than real.

LIFE IN BERTINORO

Attico and I began to get to know the town that for a few years would become our own. Little streets, the butcher, the tailor, and so many other little shops precisely facing the main road, which was pompously named the Corso. The same jovial exuberance emanated from everywhere and from everyone. Many children joined up with us, friendly, and perhaps a little fascinated by us.

On one side of the town hall's piazza, and in front of the only hotel, there was a strange monument. It was a tall column standing out against the sky, and around it were anchored big rings, where each ring corresponded to one of the town's families.

This represented a Hospitality Column. In ancient times the knights passing through Bertinoro would tether the reins of their horse to one of those rings. Automatically they would become welcome guests of the corresponding family.

We didn't tether any horse. But we were welcomed, loved and protected by all the inhabitants, who made us feel an integral part of the town. We got used to their exuberant happiness, and we were no longer just tolerated. We experienced their solidarity, understanding, and respect.

Eventually we tasted once again what it was like to no longer feel like foreigners in our own homeland of Italy.

We started going to school again. I went to elementary school. Attico, as a first year middle school student, presented a new problem: Bertinoro had only the elementary school and Attio would need to attend the middle school in another town, For-

limpopoli. Mamma maintained that going there was too dangerous. The bombings were always more frequent and the middle
school was there along the Via Emilia road.

With Papà still far away and impossible to contact, Mamma on
her own made an irrevocable decision. Attico would need to
enter into the seminary.

My brother's reaction was of absolute disagreement, but fortunately in those times the authority of parents had a certain
weight. We would be able to catch a glimpse of one another only
on Sundays at Mass from now on.

The seminary was that same sad, gloomy building we had seen
on our arrival day. A high wall separated its garden from the
piazza. Early in the morning the echo of sacred chants emanated
through the air.

The fateful day arrived. In the severe atmosphere of the seminary parlor, Attico with his head low seemed to search desperately for a reason for his terrible sense of abandonment and
loneliness.

I would have caught his eyes, if only he had looked my way. I
would have liked to reassure him with a serenity that I didn't
feel, but he didn't raise his gaze. He was closing in upon himself,
keeping his desperation from growing more severe in seeing
mine, and annihilating him.

We went back outside, my mother and I. The seminary door
closed slowly and I was firmly separated from my most important point of reference. As we headed towards home, a tangible sense of solitude and absolute loss enveloped me. No more
would I have his light touch on my shoulder, no more would I
have the sense of his protection and security. I looked at Mamma
who was quietly wiping away tears.

Sundays seemed few and far between for my anxious waiting.
Then the little church came to life, overflowing with the families

of the seminarians. Those closest to the altar participated in the Mass.

I distracted myself waiting for the boys' arrival by focusing myself on the fearless maneuvers of Brunella. She would go up and down the stairs of a side chapel. She was little more than two years old and her exuberance and happiness shone through the sparkle of her eyes.

Then the light sound of footsteps and there they were, the seminarians entering the church. Like a long row of black dots they winded through a side door towards the altar. It was difficult to make out which one was Attico, all wrapped up as they were in severe black tunics.

Even his rebellious hair seemed to convey the austerity of the moment. I could feel more than see his sad expression. His hands were united in prayer, his posture composed and resigned, in strident contrast with the exuberance of his age.

No more delirious raids along the streets of the town. And I didn't go by myself, for without Attico the raids had lost all their allure.

Every now and then the seminarians went out for a walk. Their destination was predictable: the Rocca, residence of the bishop. My primary focus was waiting for this event.

They formed a long line, two by two, orderly and disciplined. In front went the youngest and the older ones followed. My attention was focused on Attico. He wore the long black tunic made less harsh by a row of red buttons and a wide red band that wrapped around his waist, finishing with notches that fell to his side, the red band waving with every step.

I concentrated on Attico's face, protected by a black hat, proud of its triumph in being able to subdue his rebellious hair. Then my long and anxious wait was rewarded. His gentle gaze, and then his hand stealthily and slowly gestured a greeting. I felt an enormous sense of peace.

And I continued going to my own school. Classes always took place despite the war. The bombings raged. If a school was damaged by a bomb, another school quickly sprang up in its place.

My teacher, Nilde Bassenghi, didn't laugh at my errors but encouraged me to do better. She spurred me to be inclined to dream, to fantasize. She shaped my imagination, which is the only haven that never abandons you. She taught me to love the poetry of the great poets, and to seek to understand that which every piece of writing may conceal.

THE WAR CREEPS CLOSER

The senseless and unrelenting war flared ever closer to us, it was on our heels, but still not enough to scare us. From the house's garden closed in by a little wall, you could overlook all of the plains that led to the sea. Rimini, Ravenna, Cesena, Cesenatico and then closer, Forlì, Ronco, Forlimpopoli: they formed a crown above the Via Emilia road.

Pre-announced by their familiar rumbling sounds, the enemy airplane formations took turns performing executions and maneuvers . Ever more numerous and frequent, they flew over Bertinoro in dives. We positioned ourselves on the garden wall, watching the airplane acrobatics. Bertinoro was spared for the moment, as objectives much more important awaited annihilation.

I stared, enraptured by the myriads of lightweight, glittering threads that rose and fell in the air. They were disruption and defense, anti-aircraft missiles neutralizing the bombs, our only protection against the warplanes.

The roar of the engines became more deafening as enemy plan formations, compact and numerous, swept in without mercy. Clusters of bombs reached the soil, ferocious and unrelenting. First there was a crashing sound followed by a column of smoke. Then flames shot up towards the sky, taking along with them beams, earth, ruins, mangled bodies, and monuments that until that moment were witnesses to a magnificent past. All reduced to formless piles of rubble.

Forlì was the city most harassed by bombs for it had a military airport. Sitting on that garden wall I was too young to understand, to find a justification or a reason why they wanted so much death, the annihilation of a civilization, of a Nation.

The days passed along and winter was almost at our door. Mamma decided to make a very quick foray back to Tuscany, as she had often hinted she would need to do. We had need of everything, especially more clothes to protect us from the cold.

Attico stayed in seminary, and Franco was entrusted to Signora Lina.

Mamma armed herself with courage and we set off: she, Brunella and I. Our destination was Monte Buono, a little Tuscan village in the middle of the mountains, near Pitigliano. The first night was rather eventful as the general situation had worsened notably. We were sometimes rushed off the train for fear of a bombing. The train was sometimes forced to stop interminably for a while. We finally arrived in Orte, then took a motorcoach towards Viterbo and finally Pitigliano.

1943: TRIP TO MONTE BUONO IN TUSCANY

In Pitigliano, I remember a long bridge and an endless row of arcades, that gave the impression of being in competition of who was more determined to keep the bridge suspended. Dark and silent streets created something ancient that hovered in the air. We saw very few people, and they seemed more interested in the past than the current. We passed along practically unobserved.

We were now on the last tract of the journey towards Monte Buono. Mamma had lived there when she was little, and she still had anchored there her most beautiful memories and her parents. But above all was the memory of her paternal aunt, Elvira, whose name she bore herself

Zia Elvira…a feminine figure who strolled in the garden of their palazzo, between the flowerbeds and among the roses and hydrangea, carrying her little parasol, speaking in a soothing voice, she was my mother's dream and sanctuary. The large palazzo where she lived rose imperiously between the mountains, the anachronistic witness of something that existed but ought not to be. These were Mamma's earliest memories…

And now to return there. We were close. We found a piazza with a bit of life. In one corner of the piazza a sign proclaimed, 'Donkey Rental', and incredulously I understood that aside from bicycles one could also rent donkeys.

Mamma with a confident scowl and bold stride, enlisted a rather ancient man with two donkeys. These were the only means of covering the last stretch of the journey to Monte Buono.

I was lifted onto the donkey, holding Brunella tightly against my chest. Then it was Mamma's turn. She gave one look around the piazza, then in a dignified voice pronounced, "I will get on at the first clearing after the piazza." It would have been humiliating for her to mount a donkey in the piazza, so she chose to wait.

We were on our way. I was fascinated by the new adventure, trying to match my sway to the pace of the animal. I stopped trying after a short while because it was too difficult.

We ventured into a thick forest on a road that seemed more imagined than real for how poorly marked it was. After a while we came to a small clearing in the forest. There began a momentous undertaking that I can recall. The man undertook a thorough and meticulous study of the earth, in search of a boulder or of some elevation of land that could facilitate Mamma's climb up onto the donkey. After a careful inspection, he identified a big rock sticking out from the side of the road,

A sigh of relief came from the donkey owner's chest. Here we have it, he thought, and pulling the donkey with the reins he managed to position the stubborn animal at the rock. Mamma approached, wary. She rested her hands on it to be certain of its stability and tried to get on. A jump and her strangled cry, "The beast is moving!"

A new solution was studied, this time to secure the donkey's head firmly to a tree while its owner pulled the donkey's tail tightly to stabilize it. Comfortably seated in the saddle, I scrutinized the man's face. He had an amused expression and was trying desperately not to laugh. He had turned a job into a hilarious interlude.

Mamma declared that the donkey's tethering wasn't working. Meanwhile, tightly lashed to the tree, the donkey pronounced all of its indignation and dissent with screeches and a prolonged braying.

The man freed the donkey. The donkey, to protest having been tethered, gave two kicks at the tree. The poor man approached Mamma, and with his gaze lowered, creasing his threadbare hat, he said,

'I'm sorry, Signora, there remains only one thing to do to resolve the situation. I would need to kill the donkey. But I am so fond of him, and also I know that here in Pitigliano dead donkeys can't walk.'

He took up the reins and our little caravan departed once again. Mamma walked behind us, her step unsure, her speed slower. She exerted all kinds of special maneuvers so as not to fall. Considering Mamma's phobia of water, our fordings of little brooks bordered on a bravery even more pure, a courage even more heroic.

We passed deserted countrysides and small parcels of land borrowed from the woods. It was a land that did not know opulence, only the desperate will to be alive.

Then finally there was Monte Buono, a small cluster of modest houses, a very simple place. The lightly veiled derision of the donkey owner had been transformed along the way into unbridled admiration of Mamma's endurance on the long walk. He squeezed Mamma's little hand in his calloused ones and said, 'Signora, you are not city folk after all, you are one of us.'

I now entered into an unfamiliar environment. Life in this land had cruelly meant survival based on a pastoral lifestyle. The people here had a simple life rooted in basic day to day needs. They were a rather coarse populace, their feet well anchored to the ground, aliens to any useless sentimentality. And from their hardness they had created a shield of defense against the bitterness of life.

My maternal grandmother was one of them, strong and decisive.

Her joy in seeing us was not an exultation of embraces, kisses, or exclamations of joy. Instead she approached us calmly, her quivering lips betrayed her long pent-up emotion.

For me, then and even now, she represented protection, a rock that nothing could scratch. In her I saw Mamma.

She manifested all of her love knitting sweaters, socks and blankets in continuation. All of the women participated, and speedily, but my interest was most focused on an old lady who threaded the wool.

Up high, affixed to a rod was a cloud of white wool. From this hung a thin thread hooked to a wooden tool, the spindle. With expert motions they made it spin on itself, and from the fluffy cloud of wool they created a long thread

I wanted to learn and the lady patiently indulged me. I began to spin little balls of wool from the still uneven thread. They gifted me a spindle which to me was a treasure, a tangible memory that even today I carry inside me.

I had the silent, adoring admiration of the children. My fluttering little red dress, my city shoes, and my blonde hair tied back with a showy red bow elicited a certain uproar.

I was so completely different from those other little girls bundled up in heavy and shapeless skirts, their feet imprisoned in heavy shoes. Their hair was almost always in a braid, protected with a handkerchief knotted under the chin to capture even the smallest lock of hair.

A variegated following of little girls and boys trailed me constantly. Their excited eyes were full of wonderment, seasoned with a pinch of envy. I tried to play with them. I would have liked to have had on my feet heavy shoes like theirs so as to be able to run and jump in the fields. In my heart I was one of them. But they didn't accept me, and I understood their unease. My visit was too short. I would have only poisoned their serenity.

1943: ARMISTICE AND RETURN TO BERTINORO

The war, or better yet its echo, bounced off the little village. There there were no strategic targets to hit, or roads of vital importance. An old radio squawked of faraway tragedies, of victories more dreamed than real.

Mamma would listen with trepidation to the war developments, her ear glued to the radio. She was listening to that radio on that infamous day, September 8, 1943, when tears gushed from her eyes, copious and unstoppable, and a waxy pallor contorted her face with infinite pain.

The radio had announced the unconditional surrender of Italy.

The clickety clack of the needles came to a stop, and the distressed faces of the women looked toward Mamma. The questions everyone immediately had went unasked, for no responses were possible.

"I must depart immediately, I risk being separated from Attico and Franco, I risk never seeing them again! Italy no longer exists."

Her desperation spread, contaminating everyone.

"I beg you all to help me, I must depart immediately. Every minute lost may be disastrous."

A rambling and chaotic frenzy was unleashed in order to scrape together everything possible for the journey back. An old peasant man offered to accompany us to Pitigliano.

I was lifted onto the donkey, holding Brunella tightly. I prepared myself for the agonizing procedure we had already experienced upon our arrival. But when I turned toward the second donkey, Mamma was already enthroned on the saddle. Erect and proud, she grasped the reins with confidence. A little hat kept back her blonde hair, revealing clearly her pale face. Her eyes were no longer sweet, no longer little reassuring pools.

A dark foreboding loomed over all of us. Our farewells with our grandmother and the other ladies melted a bit the souls who had made hardness their defense. There were kisses and hugs, and timid wishes of 'arrivederci', which means "until we see each other again", wishes more gestured than felt.

Not one of them believed that we would ever be seen again.

And so we left. Mamma urged her donkey along, begging it for a faster pace. I looked at her and in my child's eyes her little hat became a shiny helmet. I no longer was seeing my mother on a donkey but an indomitable Joan of Arc riding a fiery white horse.

The journey seemed to me much shorter this time. Pitigliano, Viterbo, Orte, and finally the station where we would take the train. There was a multitude of people and so many soldiers, grasping to every protuberance of the train, its doors, handles, and windows.

Italian men in uniform wandered around, stumbling without any more hope, deprived of every frame of reference as they roamed stunned and incredulous. Their pride in being soldiers had been trampled, they had been betrayed by those who should have defended them, stripped of almost every human dignity.

Very few trains were departing. Most trains that arrived didn't stop at all, as they were already overloaded with defeated human beings who had remaining only a hopeless yearning to save themselves.

But not everyone had forgotten their Christian compassion. A group of young soldiers assisted our repeated attempts to board a train that had stopped and was now departing. They surrounded us to protect us and one held Brunella. They worked together in that chaotic situation and between kicks and pushes they lifted us up on the departing train, making sure to include with us all of our baggage.

These were young men who in the general chaos had maintained and exhibited principles that today would be considered quaint. It was rare in a context where most people were living without compassion and without restraints on compulsive behavior, for the only goal most people had in that disorder was survival at any cost.

We didn't even count our bags. The hope of reuniting with Attico and Franco seemed ever more remote. We saw Bertinoro as incredibly far away, and our hopelessness only increased.

The train moved slowly. Some soldiers squeezed together to make room for us, they shielded us, protecting us - me, Brunella and Mamma, who, drained of every effort, collapsed into her seat.

Mamma thanked them and a glimmer of hope illuminated her smile.

If, in that atmosphere of chaos, of total collapse, there still existed, even if small, even if in a minority, the sense of honor and of protection of those who are weak, then Italy is not dead, and would be reborn.

The train proceeded along sluggishly, ignoring practically all the stations. Stops would have aggravated the situation. In Florence a bomb siren cut through the silence, putting in doubt the hypothetical end of the war. And the siren meant we had to quickly get off the train.

With everyone rapidly disembarking from the train, the station underpass was soon swarmed by desperate souls without their bearings. Nameless men wore military uniforms that were no longer a symbol of the Nation and belonging, but tattered and stripped of any military reference. These were men in search of lost identity.

We found a little space under the shelter of a column.

Soon, night fell. The only certainty we had was that the train had stopped. Little hope existed that it, and we, would continue the journey. Hope was baseless, considering the situation.

My mother sat down on the ground, Brunella between her arms. A soldier made some room for me between Mamma and him. I raised my gaze towards his face. He had a long beard and narrow hands one resting on the other, seeking a strength that no longer existed. His eyes were lowered towards those useless hands.

I looked down at the pavement. The uncleanliness of it gripped my stomach, filth was everywhere. I squeezed Mamma's hand trying to ignore what I was sitting on, I looked again at the soldier who with his collar raised and his legs crossed tried to hide his shabby shoes.

I fell asleep. At some point I was wakened by Mamma's voice calling me, and I came back to reality. There were comings and goings of panicked people, a thousand whys. The war had not finished. The only positive thing was that the train might be able to continue its journey.

Still only partially awake, I was resting my head on the shoulder of that soldier. Where would he be now? I have often asked myself in the arc of my life if that boy managed to survive. And if ever, every now and then, he remembered that little blonde girl who didn't have the courage to say to him, "Thank you."

We departed again, and breathed the air of total destruction. Finally we reached Forlì - or more accurately said, that which remained of Forlì. There were no more houses, just piles of rubble. Homes torn to pieces revealed their collapsed insides. That which had been at one time the sacred space of families had been violated.

The Forli station was teeming with people in agitated movements, loading any type of transportable object on every type of makeshift vehicle.

And thus had begun the timeless sport of grabbing every sellable thing.

The aeronautic barracks had been completely pillaged. Blankets, sheets, cauldrons full of shoes, furnishings - all merchandise was sold with a notable profit. The future national wealth and free market was born.

Above all of this in Forli ruled the bell tower of San Mercuriale, jutting up towards the heavens, almost a challenge to total destruction around it. Like a symbol of God and His admonishment, it was only anachronistically a wholesome sentry, silent and powerless as it was in the face of the human filth that surrounded it.

The last piece of our journey was from Forlì to Bertinoro on the Via Emilia, with a few detours here and there to go around bombed out sections of the road. Then in the distance we saw Bertinoro.

Finally we reached home and I began to have hope that my little world would be able to put itself back together.

BACK IN BERTINORO

Home...but there a bitter surprise awaited us. Germans who camped out in the piazza across from the seminary had taken over the closest house for use as a pantry. And that house happened to be ours.

A legion of famished men, emaciated and at the limits of human resistance. Around eleven o'clock in the morning they began to form a long line in front of the front door. With a resigned wait, disciplined gestures, and calm voices, they made sure their behavior shone with dignity and pride. Even if their uniforms had lost every decent shape and were falling apart and torn, they were there, to witness the honor it was to be part of a Nation.

One by one they approached. Each individual mess tin was filled with some colorless steaming schlop that for some time had lost the slightest hint of aroma. A black bread, well marked with the date that it had been baked, was put under their arm. The lid of the mess tin would hold that which was the end of the meal, a piece of salami cut with millimetric precision, and a ladle of malodorous mush, milky in appearance. And then back towards the encampment. Everything happened in a silence more complete and disciplined than I have ever witnessed.

Bertinoro remained whole to that which it had always been, a hospitable people fundamentally good.

One evening, a horse died in the encampment. It lay on the ground without any more dignity, broken down and teeming with flies. Its glassy eyes stared towards nothing. I found it difficult to imagine it could have ever been agile and quick, or proud of its usefulness.

The next morning there was no longer a dead horse but a shapeless pile of skin. During the night it had served to feed those poor soldiers at the limits of their strength.

Many people in the name of compassion faced their fears. The townspeople up until that moment had not had any problems with those soldiers. They were their allies, they had shared with us the discomforts of war. It is difficult to understand how all of a sudden an ally can transform into an enemy, and how an enemy can change from persecutor to liberator.

One by one, the townspeople began to leave provisions of every type near the German encampment, always with the fear of being labeled traitors. Above all they left bread, a food that in Emilia Romagna is never lacking.

Then suddenly the situation turned upside down. The ideological convictions, the sense of honor, the rebellion against order, the solidarity and protection of the truth, everything changed. For now Radio London squawked continually and contributed to foment encouragement and to disavow all that up to that point seemed right.

Discontent slithered around, each person knew fear and mistrust, every one could be a potential enemy.

Radio London itself agitated crime and disobedience. The insinuation was that any type of atrocity was an acceptable means to become liberated men, it was permitted and promised an idyllic future. Little by little, Radio London crackling along unleashed the worst part of so many people.

The minority, those for whom values were stronger than any pandering, became marginalized and persecuted. They were constrained to leave their town and their home, and they began to hunt men, the same men that up until that point had been considered not only friends but allies, a ruthless and persistent hunt with no holds barred.

They forgot that a soldier must follow orders. Every German became supreme evil, an unscrupulous assassin with the sadistic brutality of those who kill for pleasure.

They didn't speak any more about the enemies who bombed Italy to annihilate it, but about allies who were sacrificing their lives in the name of a phantom freedom. Freedom, a pretentious name unknown to most, made us feel tied to something great and extraordinary.

One morning a long procession of emaciated men with their uniforms and scraps departed Bertinoro. Silently the Germans had begun their retreat.

The house where we lived was next to an old building, massive and dark. It had once been a prison and then had become a house. They used to say that Mussolini was imprisoned for political reasons in that prison, a long time ago before the war. There he had become close friends with Nenni, sharing the same political creed, the same socialist faith, the same youthful impetuosity. A deep friendship was established between those two young men. Based on reciprocal esteem, their friendship was never abandoned even when their political paths parted ways.

1943: RISE OF THE RSI, REPUBBLICA SOCIALE ITALIANA

In front of the old prison was a wide open space with some little trees. It had become an informal soccer field. One day the local boys were playing soccer on that field. Happy shouts and pronounced laughter rang out amidst the thuds of the soccer ball against the walls of the neighboring houses.

Suddenly there was a total silence, a general flight, a warning. At the base of the hill appeared three enemy soldiers who began a search. But they stopped a bit to enjoy a spectacle that was rather out of the ordinary.

The boys were now safely hidden in the complex of tunnels under the old prison. But the ball which the boys had abandoned started to be kicked around by the sisters, mothers, aunts, and friends of the boys. The same thuds and shouts replaced, cleverly, those created by the boys just a short time before. With well-executed direction they began to pass the ball around and without even meaning to, started the first female soccer team.

The outcome of the soldier's haul was always failure there, for the grapevine was an absolutely effective warning.

Days of general chaos followed, alternating between fear and hope. Then the announcement came. The war was continuing and young men were being called to arms. The new Italian army had been born, the 'RSI'.[7]

Thousands of Italian boys in an act of supreme sacrifice chose to enlist. There were neither expectations nor hopes, only the heroic attempt to put back together the trampled scraps of Italy's honor.

The yearning for combat infected even the youths of Bertinoro. They had become bored of hanging out on the little wall of the piazza just to see who would arrive on the bus. Instead, the boys began to consider the prospect of changing the direction of their lives, they had a desire for stronger emotions and actions.

Many found themselves in a dilemma of what to do. Would everyone would go together? Would they be leaving childhood friends behind? Some without hesitation chose the new army.

The little wall of the piazza ended just under a stately house. On the ground floor of this house was a small type of grocery, if you want to call it that. It was one of those little stores that you can't specify exactly what type of place it is - a bit grocery, a bit living room, a bit news source. A place where local chat and news was exchanged. "They say that…" "You know that…" "It's true that…"

I remember the owner because Mamma had a store credit with them as we did our shopping there. At first glance he didn't seem very benevolent, all bundled up in a long gray shirt, but his smile indicated what kind of person he was. His smile emanated a quiet tranquility wrapped in reality. He had all the positive traits of a good Emilia Romagna man.

When I would go into the store, he would smile and greet me with, "Buongiorno Signorina Persimmon."

Winking and amused, he would ask me, "How many persimmons today?"

Persimmons were a fruit I hadn't known before Bertinoro, but which had become my passion.

He was pleasant and always helpful. Once during a machine attack in the piazza he restrained my anxiety to run home. He held me in a corner of the shop, saving me from my childish recklessness. The machine gun crackle was persistent but his strong arm held me back. I remember him like that, good and altruistic.

This man had two children, a boy and a girl. The boy was an inveterate regular of hanging out on the piazza wall. The secret meetings of the boys became ever more lively, should we enroll in the RSI or should we hide out?

The grocer's son was a tenacious reader of Gordon, the masked man and other similar men that passed via various books from one hand to another. Soaked in heroism and overflowing with love of country, he was convinced to go with the nascent new army.

He decided, like a good son, to talk to his father about it, which was commendable and necessary. It was a widely shared logic.

The ramifications of that conversation were deafening. The decision they boy expressed to his father was like lightning from a calm sky. Over the years I have replayed the scene in mind based on what I heard happened.

The boy was like so many, who during the dinner hour, decided to talk with his parents. His mother was dedicated to the family. Small in stature, she went out rarely, and was always accompanied by her young daughter. The daughter had delicate features and a delightfully harmonious figure, with a confident gait that only an interior tranquility can give.

"Papà," said the boy, "I have decided to enlist in the RSI."

There was a grave silence, a quiet and pained dismay. The voice of the father broke the silence.

"But you are betraying our ideals! All of our family have always been faithful socialists, and we are respected for our consistency. But we see Mussolini as a traitor who has repudiated our roots." His trembling voice was testimony to his absolute faith in more just arguments.

The father convinced his son to go into hiding. Rumba, for that became the boy's battle name, left soon thereafter.

The boys on the wall were split for the first time in their lives. Some hoped to save the honor of Italy in the RSI. Others, like Rumba, hoped to save Italy via the rebellion.

And so arose the first partigiani ("partisan") teams. A few hid themselves in the mountains, although it certainly took a lot of courage and just as much fantasy to define Monte Cappuccino as a mountain. It was a little upland in the shelter of Bertinoro,

A little road snaked upward to the summit in just a few minutes. There sat an old convent, testimony of an ancient history. Along the road were trees, or really elder bushes, accustomed more to amorous rendezvous than to heroic gestures. A few cypresses were there to remember the sacredness of the place.

On the right hand slope was a villa with an enclosed park. This possessed all the characteristics of a safe hiding place, but I believe that the fearless Rumba had never slept outdoors, as he had better options available to him.

Comfortable farmhouses, libations drunk with the marvelous and fragrant Albana wine, amorous embraces eager to please, the absolute assurance of not being betrayed and the adoring admiration convinced him of being undefeatable.

A good part of the population resurrected the legend of Passator Cortese - a national Robin Hood type who had stolen from the rich to give to the poor. Rumba modernized it all, promising freedom and ransom from the fascist tyranny.

He financed it by extorting poor people, and there was born his strength of self-financing. Rumba of course was protected, and continued to maintain contact with his family.

At a certain point, Rumba tired of going from one farmhouse to the other. He revealed his latest plans to his parents during a short visit. These plans would create a turning point in the quality of his career. He announced to them that he was planning an attack. He would demonstrate his heroism and his creed via an eye-catching deed: to go down into town and kill the patrol that every evening swept through the streets of Bertinoro.

Rumba's father was mortified and tried to explain the inevitable consequences of such a gesture. He ordered Rumba to stay hidden and to avoid any type of criminal act. He illustrated with a concerned voice that we were in war, that to kill a German or a fascist would have uselessly triggered a series of tragic demands.

In war there exist precise laws. Retaliation would be unleashed immediately, and for every German killed, ten or more hostages, even if innocent, would pay with their execution by firing squad.

With desperation and an anguished voice, he begged his son to desist. He said, "Look, you have to see, we would be the first ones chosen as hostages, the first to be shot. Don't be the assassin of your own family!"

Rumba lowered his face and at first he seemed convinced. But the expression on the faces of his father, his mother, and his sister betrayed an ominous anguish.

The new government moved in. It established a minimum of order and organization. And the Germans continued their slow retreat.

RETURN OF PAPÀ

One day, we were finally able to embrace our papà again. He returned like a bleached copy of the Papà that I had last seen. He had become a being stripped of every vigor, no longer proud, no longer hopeful for the future. Only despairing of an uncertain tomorrow.

He was hesitant to talk about his troubled adventures. Not talking about them helped him to forget them. He told us only that he was deported from that which had been his world, Rhodes, and taken to Germany. He was considered an enemy by those who in that moment had become very bitter foes thirsty for reprisal. He was catapulted into a culture that he didn't understand and which had wiped out all of his beliefs. The little strength he had remaining had been conserved in order to find his family, the only point of reference and hope.

The war raged more ferociously than ever. Bombings followed one after the other in a persistent rhythm.

Bertinoro was no longer the weak spectator of that which was occuring down on the plain, but had become an integrated part of the total devastation.

By day there was a coming and going of planes piloted by our new English and American "friends" who were already aware of their force and power. Nighttime became a psychological war. A single plane flew over the region in a continual drone, a slow and merciless flight. Its task was to keep fear alive during the night-time hour when even a brief sleep could help you forget the war. The airplane was called Pippo, and it tormented us all the way until the end of the war.

Meanwhile those who had once been cruel enemies had now become liberators, allies, friends. Before becoming our friends they had even thought about the children, those who would tomorrow become the new generation, those who in their cheerful innocence still believed in good.

In addition to bombs they alternated blasting objects more varied, unknown, and consequently attractive. Feathers, toys, and so many others aroused curiosity and desire for possession. Immediately they accomplished their desired goal. When the child attempted to get it, there was suddenly a deafening boom and there went a little angel up to heaven. Those who were able to survive carried a mark of blood that moment, never forgotten.

The bombings were continuous. The Anglo American front had stopped in force just a few kilometers from Bertinoro, on the bank of the Ronco river. Their strategy was to smooth the road with any means in order to facilitate the advance.

Bertinoro had become the preferred target. They raged upon it with unprecedented and unjustified ferocity. In the whole town there were only a few soldiers, very young boys really, who patrolled the streets. These boys helped to remove the rubble, and they did it for their patriotism and ideals.

By now fear and mistrust had infected everyone and everything. This mix generated barely controllable and highly explosive atmosphere.

It was the perfect moment for Rumba to write his own name in the history of Italy.

RUMBA ESCALATES HIS CRIMES

Under cover of night, with darkness as his accomplice, he came down from a nearby farmhouse. He hid behind the staircase overlooking the little church of San Rocco. It was a safe place with a perfect view and a strategic placement due to its guaranteed escape.

He heard the sound of a light footstep, the night patrol. The patrol's only goal was to instill a little security and lawfulness. And yet Rumba struck without pity. Young soldiers barely more than 18 years old crumpled from the shots. Two died. One was struck gravely and carried to the house of a doctor who lived nearby.

The doctor tried to save the boy wounded by Rumba, transforming his kitchen into an operating room, but it was useless. The soldier died. The doctor, with his tremendous value for human life, respected the oath imposed on him by his profession. But he was later pursued, and charged with being a traitor, forced to live abroad. The doctor's name became first on the list of traitors to eliminate.

Having completed this massacre, Rumba, like any good megalomaniac, initialed it with a theatrical gesture. He left on top of the martyred bodies his hat, which had a showy red star.

The reprisal was unleashed punctually and unavoidably.

Ten hostages were taken from their houses. First, Rumba's father, his brothers, and other relatives both close and distant. All of them had been steadfastly anti-fascist. Their salvation would be offered if the person responsible for the attack turned himself in. This invitation was repeatedly offered as is written in the law.

The appeal was absolutely ignored. The known and feared person responsible, Rumba, did not turn himself in.

The hostages were lined up under the wall of the piazza and shot.

They maintained their dignity all the way until death, in the same way that in life they had sustained their political faith. They died, innocent, because of a person whose goal was ambition, a person who lacked any human morals. Rumba.

Few of the local population participated in this internal war. By now the few Germans who remained in town were camped out in the park of Villa Prati. They didn't feel very safe anymore, the hostility was clear and tangible. But they too were so young, and the desire to socialize was stronger than fear. Or they simply still believed in human goodness.

In the piazza of the town hall there was the only bar in town. The owner, Signora Vienna, was respected and well known by all. She tried desperately to stop what then happened, and for this she was compelled to flee and continued to be persecuted even after the war.

I remember one event with total clarity. I was coming out of the church after catechism classes. I saw two very young Germans, barely more than boys, stopped by three or four other men. These other men seemed to be smiling and friendly, they offered the Germans glasses and pats on their shoulders. They encouraged the young Germans to drink, offered a toast and paternal smiles. The two young men, reassured by such cordiality, headed back towards the camp.

But they would never arrive.

Their bodies wound up in a ditch, eyes wide open towards a sky incapable of facing such cruelty, riddled by silent and careful shots from behind.

It takes a certain type of courage to strike someone who looks you in the eye, and that type of courage was missing in these assassins.

There was another search, another futile appeal for the culprits to turn themselves in. Then more innocent people were taken away and shot to death as reprisals for the culprits' crimes.

MOVING TO THE BOMB SHELTERS

And the bombings continued. Incessantly. The war stormed ahead, giving the best of its sad bag of tricks. Staying in town became too dangerous. My parents decided that Franco, Brunella in her pram, and I would need to spend the daylight hours near or inside a shelter.

At the top of Bertinoro beyond the castle, the bishop's seat, there was a large pyramid. I had never known why it was in that particular spot nor for what purpose it had been built. It was identified as an object difficult to spot and as security for possible safety. At its feet was dug a type of cavern and in that cavern many children sought refuge.

There was word going around that the Germans, in order to slow the advance of the enemy, had transformed our little town of Bertinoro into an impregnable, heavily mined fortress. It seemed to represent the last obstacle for the Angloamerican advance, and for this reason all the ferocity of the bombers concentrated on Bertinoro.

I saw Attico only on visitors' day, as the seminary boys remained shut inside the seminary the rest of the time. Their walks had been abolished, as being outside was deemed too dangerous. Prayers were intensified from dawn to sunset, in search of the attentions from a God who seemed to have lost every authority, a God harassed by a thousand Why's.

One morning a bomb directly hit the farmhouse a few meters

from our shelter. The air pocket flung us one upon the other in a whirlwind of earth, stones and desperate yells. Then finally silence.

The most atrocious spectacle appeared before our eyes. In the total panic everyone including my parents were terrorized. The farmhouse had been reduced to a pile of smoking ruins. That which had been the barn, a place of peace and serenity for the harvest, a dance floor for happy youths and excursions of chickens, chicks, and bellicose geese, was now a battlefield.

Fortunately the farmers were safe for at the time of the bombing they had been in the fields, far from home. Otherwise the earth was soaked in blood, and miserable animal remains hung from bushes. A cow lay half covered by rubble that seemed to try to hide the macabre atrocity of its haphazard position.

The pyramid stood out in one piece, but our shelter had partially collapsed. Mamma loaded packages containing the most important necessities while Papà took Franco piggyback and I pushed Brunella in her pram. We headed out among the continued hissing of bombs and blasts towards another shelter, this one dug out under the seminary. There we would find Attico.

Finally we arrived at the new shelter, a repurposed cistern. The experience of the partially collapsed shelter we had just left made the new shelter appear to us like a salvation. It was dug out from the right side of the town wall of Bertinoro and one accessed it from an opening on the side. There was a fairly wide room whose sides had long protuberances, like long benches. Then as the room narrowed it became a tunnel that climbed upwards into a tightly formed curve. After a few meters more you would arrive in a high circular room, just under the garden of the seminary.

To get to the garden you had to climb a ladder that to me seemed incredibly tall, but it was the only possible way out other than the side of the town wall. And only for anyone with the courage to climb all the way to the opening, since the ladder climb was so narrow that no light at all seeped in.

Little by little the shelter filled up beyond its capacity with various groups of people. Another group of townspeople. The seminarians. The teachers. Then all of a girls' boarding school. So many little girls who remained without word from their families, so many teachers crushed by their superhuman responsibility.

People wandered afraid, they took up half of the cistern with suitcases and packages. They were trying to save everything that they felt connected them to their families. And there was always the unspoken fear of perhaps, someday, or already, no longer having a family.

In one corner were huge jars of marmalade and packages of crackers so hard that they could serve only as spoons to scoop out the marmalade.

The cistern was busy with active comings and goings of people. There was a continuous rummaging inside the packages and the suitcases . A chaos of objects was scattered on the ground, and often things were only able to be found when a little ray of light arrived and allowed them to be seen.

The night was the worst part of the ordeal. The only way to safety was the little window about six meters above the ground, and the long ladder would become practically invisible. Physiological needs required acrobatic bravery, and naturally a very few were able to manage this. All the others in little groups ventured to the exit of the shelter during the day, confronting the bombs. Hardly anyone chose the nighttime with its hidden dangers, walking around where you could end up falling off a cliff.

Everyone tried to set themselves up as best they could. Due to his nimbleness, my father was able to easily climb the ladder. He would then cross the garden of the seminary and go to our house, trying to maintain a certain normalcy. He would prepare something hot for us to eat, and then, using the intervals between one bomb and another he would find his way back to the shelter. These forays became always more dangerous, but Papà continued, undaunted.

There were very few men in the shelter, they would rush there only if it was required that they render themselves useful. Papà, as a man and a soldier, coordinated aid when help was requested. He helped to free the streets of rubble and to bring help to those who had need.

A bomb directly struck the only hotel in town, shaving it to the ground. Fortunately the owner's wife and children were with us in the shelter. But the owner himself had remained in the hotel to protect his life's work, what would have been the future of his children.

His relatives dug with any tool available, using bloodied and panicked hands with the remote hope of finding him still alive. It was not to be.

His son wanted to bring the news himself to his mother and sister, who were still holding out hope. The son appeared at the entrance of the shelter, a figure covered in dust. His hands rested along his sides which were red with blood, his mouth trembled to hold back a despondent sorrow. Sorrow was the only expression on his petrified face marked with furrows, and in these furrows flowed copious and unstoppable tears.

Silently he grasped in a forlorn embrace all that remained in his world, his mother and his sister. There were neither words nor cries, just a mute and at the same time deafening grief, like the thunder of that brutal bomb.

Papà continued his forays outside, indefatigable he would go out and come back, bringing that which Mamma requested. Pressed by those inside with a thousand questions about the situation outside, he responded with calm words seemingly memorized. Concealing the actual situation outside, he tried to transmit to us a serenity that he had not had for a long time.

'Everything is ok, Elvira, everything is alright. Try to be calm, in a few days we will return home. Focus on taking care of the children.'

His serenity gifted us with the conviction that nothing bad could ever happen to our Papà.

Then one day he came back earlier than usual. There were no questions, he put his hand on Mamma's shoulder and said, 'I'm sorry, Elvira, a bomb has directly struck our house. I had just that moment left and the blast threw me to the ground, and with me the boiled potatoes that I had prepared.'

His calm and perhaps illusory serenity managed to convince us that the loss of the potatoes was perhaps the greater evil.

That day we ate sandwiches that had been scented with anise, which Mamma had prepared earlier in the event of an emergency.

All day Papà went back and forth trying to salvage what little remained at the house, and was late coming back to the shelter.

Early in the evening, while Mamma tried to calm her apprehension as to why Papà was late, she did not realize that Attico had disappeared. She thought it was just a momentary departure, and she asked everyone if they had seen him. The seminarians, flooded with questions from Mamma, responded that yes, they had seen him go through the exit at high speed.

Papà finally arrived, dirty and pale, aware that the worst thing might be the next attack. He looked at us and asked, 'Where is Attico?'

Everyone wanted to be together, everyone needed to be together. So many people, away from the inferno of the bombings outside, people who had left the other shelters that were already no longer safe, piles of rubble that already were taller than the remaining houses. In a flash, my father was no longer there, he had gone out in search of Attico.

Mamma was mute and with her hands on her face she understood. Attico had gone looking for Papà. He had conquered the fear of leaving, but now he was being searched for with the same anxiety.

Interminable minutes, and eternal, atrocious images of what could have happened in that inferno of fire. But then Papà and Attico were there in front of us. My brother was so small and defenseless, his black tunic white with dust. He had lost the austere hat and his rebellious lock of hair had seen better moments. Mamma pulled him to her in a huge embrace.

Attico came over to me and gave me a light pat on the shoulder, his smile captivating and the promise that he would never again go away from us. And thus I had my own personal hero.

Now that we were all relieved, Papà told us what had happened. Not very far away, behind the shelter of a wall, a young soldier had interrupted my brother's run. The machine gun fire was flying, and the soldier had thrown Attico behind the wall and covered him with his body, holding him firmly, and thus protecting and saving him.

The days piled up one upon one another, each one full of discomfort. Even the last crumb of tenacity had been consumed, trying to hold out against sleep in order to be safe. Sleep and safety, the most yearned for and urgent needs.

We would sleep one up against the other. Near me was a young priest, Don Michelin. Higher up, towards the end of the narrow tunnel, in the most discreet and inaccessible place was the Bishop. There was a continual back and forth flow of priests who were focused on making the forced stay of the high prelate as supportable as possible.

The bishop was seated on a red armchair, which seemed ridiculous and anachronistic in that place. In the evening a curtain sought to create for him a bit of privacy. When laying down on the ground, we occupied the whole curve of that narrow tunnel.

In the evening everyone was ordered to line up one next to the other. But since the ground was slightly sloped upward, waking up was rather eventful, you needed to be a tightrope walker to untangle yourself and stand up.

By now Bertinoro was deserted. The Germans were marching northward. Two soldiers still remained. They had positioned two machine guns under the wall of the castle's perimeter. Protected by the wall and running along it, they fired those weapons giving the impression that not just two soldiers but an entire army was present. Thus they held in check for several days the hardened and invincible Anglo American army which was confirmed to be on the other side of the little Ronco river.

The enemy was still determined to raze Bertinoro to the earth, considered to be a last bastion, an impenetrable fortress, completely laden with explosive mines.

At this point Rumba, the good partigiano hero, would have needed to act as Robin Hood to salvage that little that remained.

But making nighttime attacks striking behind one's back is one thing, while confronting openly an enemy army was quite another. And so he preferred to leave his fellow citizens under continued bombings, maintaining that it was too dangerous to intervene.

After close discussions, and at the limits of human strength and without any more provisions, the adults present in the shelter decided to form a small delegation to reach the military posts on the other side of the Ronco river. They would reassure the army that the conquest of Bertinoro would be certain, and there were no mines but only civilians who were exhausted, dirty, hungry and anything but menacing.

It was decided that three men would go. One elderly man, then young Don Michelino who in his cassock was an indicator of sincerity and moral integrity, and thirdly my father who wore his military uniform, always a symbol of dignity and honor.

They departed at the first sign of evening twilight, at dusk. They sought the entrance of the aqueduct that went along Monte Cappuccino, which provided drinking water to all the houses and the countryside. It was certainly not an easy walk inside the aqueduct, lit up by a little flashlight. Some parts were the height of a man and other parts were so low that it required them to walk bent over.

Every now and then the aqueduct pools were full of water, which they had to cross via crumbling bridges, and always with the fear of encountering some insurmountable obstacle. Then finally the first dim light of dawn, and just a few instants to orient themselves.

And there before them was all the might of the entire army. The three hardly aggressive looking men were suddenly surrounded.

OCCUPATION OF BERTINORO

They were taken to the commander, escorted by soldiers with weapons in hands. To explain their mission was not easy, for they spoke a different language.

Don Michelino, with his long cassock like a shield, explained the goal of their mission more with gestures than words. The military faces remained rather severe. Then the elderly man stepped forward and tried to explain with unclear but colorful pantomimes that the three men had good intentions and that this wasn't a trap.

Papà saw that the outcome at this point was shaky. He showed the soldiers his documents attesting that he was a part of the Italian aeronautic military. The soldiers' attitude changed notably, and the three men were accompanied back to the entrance of the aqueduct. Finally the little delegation reentered our shelter.

Long rows of Anglo American trucks, weapons, and jubilant men swept down the Via Aberone from the village of Polenta, a stop of the divine Dante, all the way to Bertinoro. These were not emaciated men, but an army in the fullness of its glory and predominant strength.

The long road used to be lined with majestic and hundred year old sycamore trees from a time long ago, their trunks clothed in a thousand colors. No longer came the music of leafy branches moving in the wind. Instead a gloomy silence accompanied the triumphant entry of the victors. Abject stumps of trunks shredded by bombs and branches and fronds mixed with mud covered their path. And in this way Bertinoro was occupied.

Not a moment of resistance, not even one shout of joy. The soldiers chose which houses to inhabit, and we finally left the shelter.

We had lost almost any glimmer of civilization. Dirty and worn out, we passed in front of that which once had been our home. Almost completely torn to pieces you could see inside the bedroom, the window untouched, the curtains swayed in a wind indifferent to such desolation. The bathtub was enthroned like an armchair in the middle of the garden.

Slowly we worked our way towards the carabinieri barracks, climbing and descending over piles of rubble. We didn't feel joyously liberated but wretchedly hopeless.

After a long wait, they assigned us a house.

The family that had lived there before had moved to the north out of fear of retribution. It was a three story house. On the second floor was our family and the family of a carabinieri marshall, he also had been sent north for protection. The third floor hosted troops that alternated back and forth to the front.

We were not sure enough in the circumstances how to weigh the pros and cons. We had to think that that house was the only possibility to shelter us from an imminent winter. The first room had two beds, one against the other. With some imagination you could devise in the second room a kitchen. Everything was covered in dust and plaster. One kitchen wall, that once had rested against another house, now seemed to rest against a pile of rubble that was the remains of that house.

Huge cracks radiated on the walls in a braid that, if the whole situation had not been tragic, would have been rather picturesque. The biggest cracks let in blades of light and the free entry of rain and wind. As well as hordes of hungry mice.

Two windows allowed a complete view of the piazza and the infamous piazza wall. The arrival of the bus seemed to us a positive note in so much desolation. We didn't know that under those windows, unimaginable atrocities were about to occur.

On the left was a lordly mansion where the military command center and the mess hall were set up. The soldiers came and went, and trucks came in continuous movement. I have to admit that they spelled a certain calm.

Attico and I began once again our excursions, once for pleasure now for necessity. We needed to pick up eggs and anything that seemed edible from the nearby farmhouses and also wood to keep ourselves warm. The sycamore trees had their blow of mercy thanks to our hatchets.

Papà tried to make the house more habitable, he tried among all the rubble to find anything that could be useful. He spent many hours trying to close the cracks in the walls.

There were many Italian American soldiers, and one was called Ronnie. He brought us cardboard and pieces of planks. He tried to help us. One day he saw me sewing and asked me to sew for him the various tabs and ranks onto his jacket. From that moment there was a constant flow of soldiers who politely would ask me to do little sewing jobs. They tried to return the favor by always bringing me something nice. For me it was an entertainment, I didn't know I'd established child exploitation!

The day arrived for Papà to depart. He had to go to the closest airport and take up his service again. Everyone in Bertinoro knew that Papà was a soldier, but we were always helped, protected and taken care of. The people had never betrayed the thousand year old tradition of kindness, the absolute sense of hospitality.

We remained alone without Papà. Attico was promoted head of the family. I dreamed like a child and lived like an adult. Brunella lived only joy as she was too young to understand.

Franco was practically absent, closed in his world. Never a tantrum, never any obstinacy so common in children of his age. Everything he did seemed first carefully evaluated. For the rest of the children who were throwing tantrums and stamping their feet, would that have obtained something? Or a better question yet, did that thing even deserve to be obtained? In the uncertainty of the answer, he decided to save his energy and confront life with calm and resignation.

Attico and I began once again a quasi normal life with our long excursions in the nearby countryside. At every farmhouse we found the same good heart, the same joyful welcome. And we would return home drunk on cheerful feelings.

With dives into white mantles of snow, running slowed down only by sloping hills, we tried to take back a broken childhood. Moments of calm alternated with moments of fear; randomly the military trucks passing in the piazza indicated that we should close our doors and windows and remain shut inside our homes. It was unconditionally prohibited for everyone but especially for the women to appear at the window or in any way make their presence known.

But curiosity of the unknown events was stronger than any command. A procession of men never seen before wound through the piazza. Strangers appeared with heavy long gowns reaching to their feet and a band that held a long scimitar hung from their waists. We found this anything but reassuring.

These men had an appearance more savage than human. Their faces were covered by untamed beards, and they yelled with guttural and unpleasant voices in a strange and fortunately incomprehensible language. Their vulgar gestures were more than eloquent.

Escorted by armed military, with azure bands on their arm,

they were accompanied to an encampment outside town, a place rather inaccessible and isolated. Their compensation was the spoils of war, and this was taken with force, whoever it might be, man, woman, or child, enough to unleash their primordial instinct.[8]

Fortunately their visits were not very frequent, but the dark and fearful atmosphere that they left behind was very difficult to dissipate.

After the bombings and the yearned-for liberation, the Anglo American army thought respectably about our cultural reeducation. One night a week in the piazza they provided entertainment. Along the sides of the piazza the new Italian soldiers allied with the Anglo Americans lined up diligently. The new allied Italian army was called the Army of the South.

Few were very convinced, others resigned, some almost entertained. The usual protocol: the piazza filled up with people and a full Scottish band played to the delight of the soldiers and the people.

Bold and brawny boys put on elegant little skirts in garish colors. On their heads was a beret, and at their side a coquettish little purse adorned in white leather. Snow white knee socks graced their sturdy calves, where they exhibited the only masculine touch: a dagger stuffed into one of the knee socks.

They walked back and forth along the entire length of the piazza to the plaintive sound of the bagpipe with a cadenced step. Their haughty bearing was in stark contrast with the fluttering and graceful movement of the little skirts that showed off their muscular legs.

In the center, between the bagpipe players sat just one man. He was dressed the same but wore a leopard skin complete with paws and tail that swayed. With a big drum he set the beat of the band.

The music delighted us for some time. There were continued about-faces, swirls of skirts, and intense drum solos. Finally the ceremony would finish, but my curiosity did not.

Were they men or women? And if they were men why did they wear a skirt? Then the final distressing question and dilemma that remained unresolved even today, was under that skirt did they wear underwear?

The Italian Army of the South clapped furiously at the finale. I had the impression, however, that the soldiers did not quite appreciate as intended the delights of that foreign culture.

Most of the army was abandoning us, little by little. Meanwhile the liberation of the rest of Italy proceeded. There were two opposing Italian armies now: the Italian RSI in the north in a desperate defense, and the new Italian Army of the South that was trying to put back together all that remained of an Italy torn apart.

1944: FIRST COMMUNION

It was the beginning of 1944 and I was preparing for my first Communion. Mamma began searching for a white dress, or else for some fabric to sew one. The search, despite her determination, was difficult and fruitless. The stores were destroyed. She looked everywhere, Forlì, Forlimpopoli, Cesena, but everything was a pile of rubble.

The black market ruled, but only for that which was of vital necessity, especially food. The whole town rallied to help Mamma. Some ladies offered their daughters' dresses, I was too tall for my age and my body had begun to delineate the forms of that which I would become. Too tight, too short, everything was useless. I dreamed of a white dress and this desire obfuscated what ought to have been the joyous expectation of receiving Jesus.

The possibilities and all the solutions for creating a white dress were exhausted. They left Mamma sad and disappointed to not be able to give me a little dream. She opted for the only dress that had a semblance of elegance. It had been reworked, widened and lengthened, it was a blue organza. The bodice embroidered with smocking flattened the hint of my future curves. A bow in back tried to hide that the dress had been widened. By now I had resigned myself to the situation, and an abyss of hopelessness opened up.

Mamma used a leather purse, last evidence of happy times, to make some sturdy boots for Attico and me. They were precisely nailed together and certainly not appropriate for a ceremony or to go with a dress that with a lot of wishing and optimism one could define as elegant.

So she began looking for shoes, which turned out to be even more hopeless and useless than the search for the dress. Shoes wear out, and those that we found were either too small or too broken down to be called shoes. They could not be worn.

Mamma turned to the town cobbler, who had shoes that had never been picked up, or had been forgotten. There were shoes there, but those with acceptable characteristics were at least three sizes too small for me. We had to give up.

We finally opted for a pair of sky blue sandals. Mamma tried to direct my attention on the color that would go very well with the dress. I courageously overlooked the fact that they had a heel. I accepted that I should focus on the great joy of receiving Jesus. I did not look Mamma in the eyes, I knew that I would have found only much heartache.

The momentous day arrived. I got dressed slowly under the watch of Attico, Franco, and Brunella. They gave me looks of amazement and ecstatic unbounded love, and for a moment I felt happy.

All together we were off towards the church of San Rocco, only a few hundred meters away. I forced myself to walk on tiptoes to avoid the clickety clack of the heels. The road seemed endless, and the clatter of the heels' tore away any little bit of stamina I had.

There was the stairway of the church. My hand held Mamma's. Little by little I took one step up then another. There was the pressing desire to flee, and then the serious but melancholy gaze of Mamma. I walked alone towards the altar in a long row of happy children. Little crowns of flowers, and white dresses - they seemed miraculous to me. I went ahead little by little, slightly bent over to hide the tight dress.

The walk to the altar seemed endless. The clacking of the sandals boomed, the beating of my heart seemed to want to outdo itself. Under the gaze of curious faces, I sank my eyes into the lights of the altar. My tears gave a veiled tranquility to the flowers and the lights of the candles.

And suddenly I felt my feet rest lightly on the lawn of the garden in Rhodes, perfumed daisies dropped like butterflies and brushed my face, immersed as I was in those dazzling surroundings.

Jesus was inside me, in His greatness He had gifted me with imagination and fantasy. The possibility that during dark moments I could immerse myself in my unforgettable and extraordinary realm in Rhodes.

Back at the house, Mamma pulled me to her and stroked my hair. 'You will see, Piera, you will have a marvelous life and one day there will be a white dress for you.'

But my destiny held that there would never be a future white dress for me to wear with joy.

"Liberation"...and reprisal

Life continued, and so did the war. But we, having already been "liberated", were living only its echo. The future was uncertain and cloudy, the past wanted to be forgotten, and thus everyone lived for today in the grip of a euphoric general intoxication.

"Liberation" became synonymous with crime at any cost. We entered an infernal bedlam. Parental control began to teeter. Rules became obligations and requirements. Advice given for romance was often heeded but also became viewed as the cliché of parents who were too old fashioned.

Dazed girls believed in the flattery of the soldiers. They dreamed of other horizons, the American dream, no longer just a fantasy but easy to fulfill. How many girls set sail towards far off lands? Few, very few. The army went on and the girls stayed behind.

The occupation and the liberation continued, the front was pushed further north. A phase of reentry began for those who had previously fled from Bertinoro for fear of revenge and reprisal. Now people breathed a certain air of relaxation.

This relaxation, however, encouraged the false Robin Hood in the other direction. Rumba, like a truly heroic executioner, thought it would be a good idea to purify the town of fascists: true, presumed, or suspected.

In the meantime his band had notably increased. They were degenerates without scruples. They knew how to take advantage of those moments of general calm.

He would swoop into the house of the designated fascist victim. First, a beating in front of the terrorized family, then the victim silenced forever with a shot.

Often the cadaver was carried away inside a barrel, loaded onto a truck that slowly processed through town. The townspeople watched. They deplored it but stayed silent. And Rumba, unpunished, went on to become an exalted and dreaded hero.

The petitions of the families at least to have the dead body were insufficient. The body was the only sure proof of the slaughter, and he needed to make any trace disappear of who had perpetrated the crime.

In the mornings, on the terrace of Rumba's house, there swayed in the wind a safari jacket, which was the uniform he wore. For every victim he killed during the night, the uniform flapped outside in the wind.

The war was in its epilogue. Disbanded and destitute Italian soldiers roamed in search of their houses and their families, with the fear of never finding them. They followed kilometers of hardly passable roads, ambushes, and exhausting marches by night. Someone would give the returning soldiers a piece of bread or an old piece of clothing.

The hunt for the fascist soldier who was by now on the wrong side of the war had become a national sport. These soldiers didn't know and would not ever have imagined what little remaining they were to find.

What they found upon returning to Bertinoro was Rumba. He kicked off the bloodbath as a warning for those present, a lesson for those watching, and a sadistic pleasure for those who carried it out.

If the victim were a woman[9] a special treatment was reserved for her. Her head would be completely shaved and smeared with tar. Ripped apart but still alive, she was put on display to the whole town.

Rumba with the sound of the whip indicated to her to come near. She was forced to walk with her arm raised in a fascist salute, receiving blows on her back to make her walk erect if she cowered. But the most creative and savage act was left to the numerous women in the procession, women free finally to unleash their hatred and to vindicate their loved ones shot by the Germans.

The laws of war were disregarded. Pleas made to the assailants to turn themselves in were ignored.

I had never seen such savagery. The victim walked, or better said stumbled. Blood mixed with tar obscured her sight. She would fall on her knees and rise only to be greeted with kicks and punches. The female vindicators had lost any human resemblance, disheveled and screaming, they took turns spitting on the victim. The saliva mixed with blood created a repugnant trail. Usually death was more merciful than the assaults of those unrestrained hordes of attackers.

Eventually the boys began to come back to the piazza wall, those who had chosen the so-called wrong side. But the network of spies was well organized, Rumba was always kept very well informed.

The son of the miller came back too. The miller was generous and good, he never let anyone go without the fragrant aroma of bread in their home, no matter what their faction or political belief.

The miller's son had only time to greet his parents. And then the program 'Clean Italy' kicked off immediately. Every human law was left behind, friendship that had been shared within town fellowship. In the morning the young soldier was collected by a punishment delegation made up of several men. Rumba was no longer a peer and friend but an executioner, and the miller's son was just a loser to punish.

Prayers and supplications went in vain.

The whip cut through the air, precipitating on the poor soldier. The blows came one after another with a persistent and ferocious rhythm. Every so often the whip stopped, but the savagery didn't. Punches, kicks, shoves, then the whip started up again with greater violence.

Now broken, the victim initiated the spectacle, which was an exhibition and demonstration of how one should treat a dirty fascist. He had to lead the procession, staggering, required to hold the same Roman salute, his step faltering. He was accosted with kicks and punches. When his arm fell it was lifted up again with the barrel of a gun. When he fell, they lifted him up again covering him with spit. He tried to walk supporting himself on the walls of the houses, his bleeding hands groped in the desperate search for any handhold so as to not collapse to the ground. [10]

Then, he arrived in the piazza. The rage of the women with shouts and insults was reaching a climax. There the torture was finished, leaving behind what was a man just a pile of rags soaked in blood. That which remained of the young soldier was loaded into a truck, destination unknown. [11]

The Italian soldiers who had chanced fate and believed in human compassion were thereby eliminated. The fascists who had escaped at the last minute became staunch and practicing communists. And Rumba became the Godfather of Bertinoro.

Rumba's fame as a beneficent dictator was already at its peak, and his brutality was without limit. He had entered into the chosen group: a national hero, a liberator from the fascist tyranny, symbol of freedom and heroic purity. His ambition had no limits.

Rumba had become the symbol of good that triumphs over evil, proud in his safari jacket, whip in hand. He became the idol of the throngs. Loved, feared, and celebrated, he carried out sporadic sorties beyond the region's borders. Wherever there was need for a detailed cleansing via any kind of massacre, he participated as an expert. He even attained the enigma of being in more than one place at the same time.

A celebration was organized in Rumba's honor. A platform in the center of the main piazza was set up with an armchair. There

Rumba sat enthroned, entirely cognizant of his own power. With a martial air he rallied the joy of the crowd, almost all of them women. They sought to brush up against him, they kissed his hand. He was smiling and smug in his immaculate safari jacket, boots and ever present whip. He received the jubilation of a throng of people who no longer had any point of reference. They were without hope and without a future.

Rumba's notoriety increased in proportion to the crimes he committed. So much so that even other crimes were added via hearsay to the real ones. But life had to go on, and thus he decided to give the town a certain legality.

An old farmer was elected mayor. The farmer leaped at the opportunity not based on any , heroic deeds but only because he was of a proven antifascist leaning. He was one of so many who anxiously expected Stalin, dreaming of the redemption of his whole life.

And of course, the farmer took orders from Rumba. Celebrity is expensive, beautiful women and a carefree life were there at his fingertips. The town's cash register was where he could make continual withdrawals for a life ever more gilded.

This went on for some time. Then unexpectedly the farmer had a resurgence of honesty. Invoking Stalin was going fairly well and dreaming of human redemption and a better life was rational. But this could not justify cowardice and honesty.

At Rumba's umpteenth request for money, the farmer mayor resisted. He forgot his fear and greeted Rumba with pistol in hand. He ordered Rumba to not ask for any more money otherwise he would not hesitate to shoot. It was in that moment that he recognized the honor of the role that he held.

The moment was critical. The people began to think without fear, they started to evaluate the events with greater clarity. The pedestal on which Rumba rested began to teeter, to be unstable.

And so he decided to use his membership in the Resistance, the Partigiani ("partisans"), as a safeguard. To make a leap forward in quality.

Hunting fascists was no longer entertaining or lucrative. There remained few of them around anymore, and they were difficult to unearth. Most of the others had become sworn antifascists too busy to dream up a clean start otherwise.

And thus these "heroic" members of Rumba's gang, the ex-partigiani, who were in forced retirement due to lack of victims, decided to become a gang of delinquents. Experts with a license to kill, they were sanctioned by the newly minted national authority.

They kicked off a new career made up of thefts, raids, extortions, and murders. The regular activities in which they were specialized based on past experience and personal tendency. One of the members of the gang did not accept this leap in quality, for he had a morsel of honesty. He was partigiano by conviction. But he had a wife and two children. And so he decided to pull out of the group.

A vendetta was unleashed against him, cruel and senseless. During the night the gang led by Rumba broke into the house of this conspiratorial friend. There was a massacre.

In the general exhilaration, drunk on blood, the gang members neglected to notice a little four year old child hidden under the table, to whom remained only the nightmare of that which he had witnessed.

After a few years, Rumba was accused and then arrested. In a police lineup the child recognized without hesitation the perpetrator of the massacre. But that was the only crime with which Rumba was officially charged. The other crimes were considered acts of pure heroism, in the name of freedom and justice.

Rumba served just a few years of prison in Montelupo, and then once freed he took off abroad. The town of Bertinoro tried to forget and put everything into perspective. The halo went back on the head of the true Robin Hood instead of Rumba. They talked about it very little and Rumba was brought back to his just dimensions, a simple assassin. He had started his career by putting into motion that the Germans killed his father, without of course mentioning that it was hsi own fault the Germans killed his father, and without moreover mentioning that he could have saved his father by turning himself in.

But no. He moved on with unchained ambition, drunk on blood. A small, pathetic man who dreamed only of great evil.

EMILIO

The owners of the house that had hosted us returned, so we changed residences. Mamma, surprisingly festive and joyful, took up again her favorite sport: relocating.

Villa Boffondi was situated on the right hand side of Mount Cappuccino, a little outside of the center of town. On the left it bordered the Corso, the road which had once been tree lined, the road that led to Dante's little town of Polenta. There were a few houses, the school, and a little chapel dedicated to the divine Dante. The road on the right went gently uphill towards the mountain.

At the center of the fork in the road was a flower bed, by now without flowers. Even so, it added some refinement to the church of San Rocco. In the middle of the flowerbed was a little statue of the god Bacchus with a crown of grape leaves. How odd, he was there whole and festive and seemed to be a symbol of rebirth.

Little by little we returned to normalcy. Papà was transferred to Udine. Attico went to school in Forlì. I was in school at Forlimpopoli at the Magistrale Institute which Mussolini had attended in his day. The old janitor who was there in Mussolini's student days often told us about the famous student. He spoke of him with respectful pride, remembering his rebellious and resolute character.

Every morning we rushed to the piazza to jump on the bus, an old remnant of war promoted to the field of public transportation. It unloaded all its warlike bravado taking shameless advantage of the downhill stretches. On the uphill return it tried to move us to pity with shrieks, jerks and pistons.

The trip was short but extremely noisy. Laughs, pranks, the yearning to feel alive, and nascent hopes for the future. We wanted to flee from the painful memory of war. But the rubble was there, real and devastating, difficult to ignore.

Attico had met a very young soldier, Emilio, only a little older than he. He belonged to the new army, and often he came to visit us at Villa Boffondi. We played with the colored puppets he brought us. He was tall and blonde and so young it seemed impossible he had a soldier's uniform on. He didn't manage to instill in us a minimum of reverential respect. He spoke of his city Torino with love and nostalgia, his gaze veiled with emotion. He spoke of his family from whom he was no longer hearing any news.

Bertinoro had become a resting point for all the troops who were coming back from the front, and also a meeting point for the troops who instead were headed there. It was a continual coming and going. They left, and then they came back battered and embittered. They became men too soon and perhaps had never even actually been boys.

The time to go to war arrived for Emilio, he had to go to the front. He came by to say goodbye to us, a little kiss on my hair, a handshake for Attico, a pat on the cheek for Franco and Brunella. Then he was off, leaping down the stairs calm and smiling.

"I'm off to the front to receive a baptism of blood and fire, the enemy better start to shake!", he said, concealing his concern with bravura.

Mamma gave him a kiss and said, "Be careful, don't try to be a superhero."

He waved to Attico with a hand that continued to oscillate until we couldn't see him anymore.

We didn't hear any more from Emilio, it seemed that he had evaporated into thin air. We asked many people about him, then we began to fear that we would never see him again. We forced ourselves to not think about what fate he may have met.

And then one day, there he was!

He approached us unsteadily, a pale twin of the smiling and cheerful boy who had gone off to meet his destiny. He walked with crutches, slowly, his eyes lowered to make out any possible obstacle. He had only one leg.

We wanted to run away, to weep, to scream out all of our anguish. We went up to him trying to scrape together the strength to feign a calm we didn't have. He smiled at us, and gestured at the missing leg.

"I'm alive but I had to leave a piece of me behind as a hostage. I left a leg behind but I still have another."

A delicate shaking of his hands betrayed all of his despair. Quietly he recounted to us what had happened. They had to de-mine a field. Emilio had already reached a safe place and was waiting for his comrades to join him. Suddenly a boom ripped the air apart, the earth was smoking and billowing with dust. His very young commander was face down in a sea of blood. Emilio bolted towards him and picked him up. There were just a few steps to safety but closer to a treacherous and cruel destiny. An explosion. The last of the mines wanted its own moment of glory, and it stripped the carefree bravado from a true hero.

With eyes lowered he finished his account. In that moment I had the great honor of being illuminated by the glow that emanated from a genuine hero. He had gone off to the front full of faith, tall and handsome, in the flower of youth, a hymn to life. And he had become a symbol of valor, sacrificing his own life for the good of others.

Emilio, I hope that the Italy of today still maintains for you all the honor that you deserve.

REMNANTS OF WAR

The Italian Army of the South was working with the Ang-loAmericans. Or better said, they followed the orders of the liberators and were in combat on various fronts.

As they retreated, the Americans left behind various consequences, and some of these were good consequences. A certain calm, a certain order. But unfortunately they left behind also all that had served to liberate us - weapons, unexploded hand grenades and so on.

In front of Villa Boffondi there was a little farmhouse. A happy family, father, mother and a little baby girl Brunella's age, her name was Fernanda. Brunella and Fernanda played together often, running around the farmyard. The war was an occurrence too immense for toddler girls. They joyfully ran after a white lamb, who, held firm by delicate hands, tried to participate in the game by unraveling the red bows that held the little girls' hair. There was silvery laughter, shouts of festive bliss.

But one day, in the absence of her playmate, Fernanda, her chubby little face with her upturned nose, sparkling eyes, red bow, curls dancing in the wind, set out to venture a little further away. She went all the way to a big cherry tree, the juicy cherries bending the branches with their weight, so inviting but too high for little Fernanda. And there on the ground were the best cherries, those ever so slightly withered, the favorites of the little birds that had pecked them to make them fall.

Her little hand reached out for the sweet taste of the cherries. She found not succulent fruit but instead the most terrible remnant left there by the war, a little mysterious and enticing object that poked up, glittering, out of the ground.

The cherries lost all their allure, her fingers sought to extract the object from the earth There was a light pressure and then thousands and thousands of fiery splinters tore through the child, lacerating her body. They multiplied as they exploded and were increasingly fiery. It was a phosphorus bomb, a device developed not to give a sudden death but a slow, long, and torturous agony.

Fernanda...I like to believe that perhaps afterward, later on, the red bow in your hair every spring transforms into a poppy, waving in the wind, whispering your name. I like to think of you like that. Somehow it hurts less.

The yard of the farmhouse became abandoned, a black desolation, an unanswered Why.

BRUNELLA'S ILLNESS

Brunella had been born in the middle of the war, a very difficult period. You would have thought she had already abundantly paid her dues, absorbed her obliged share of pain. But at just a couple of years old she developed septic arthritis in her hip. Between highs and lows, hopes and disappointments, we prayed and we hoped.

We experienced horrible moments and continual stays in the hospitals of the towns of Cesena and Forlì, and Bologna. There were frantic searches for medicines. In those days, sulphonamides were the only remedy against infections. They appeared and then disappeared in a see-sawing supply.

Mamma spent entire nights at Brunella's bedside cradling her as she lay there so tiny and delicate, so defenseless, a helplessness that was devastating.

Mamma was always watchful and courageous beyond any limit, but resigned. She protected Brunella's life with strength and determination, opposing a very inauspicious reality. Mamma, who was afraid of the dark and afraid of water, became a force of nature because of her boundless love for Brunella.

Mamma made adventurous trips, with makeshift means, trips that could have been without return. Brunella's little face was always more diaphanous, and her little hands couldn't touch us. A little bird without wings, she fought against something that she couldn't understand, that she couldn't see.

A thousand why's were the obsession of day and night. I didn't want to pray anymore, only to curse and swear. I didn't believe in God anymore. I refused to think that a little baby had to pay for the sins of humanity. My human soul refused to believe in a God like that.

In autumn the trees reached their branches towards the sky, then spring arrived and God covered them with green leaves, the rebirth. But for Brunella?

Then suddenly a wisp of hope. Her little hands that seemed petals moved by the wind, two rose petals that brushed against her face. I drew close to her, into the nook of her neck, where there was the perfume of a nest and I found God again. Mamma seemed drained of any energy, but was smiling.

Brunella would live but would remain slightly lame.

She would know the naive sarcasm of children, the pitiful curiosity towards those who are different. From us though she would have love even more unbounded, from Mamma and Papà constant and infinite protection.

ANGLO-AMERICANIZATION

News from Papà was reassuring. He hoped to join us soon. In the serenity of the moment Mamma's passion took the upper hand, to move houses again. Bertinoro was overwhelmed by a collective hunger to forget, and instead to have fun. Dance halls proliferated like mushrooms.

The less distasteful habits which the Americans left behind changed our way of life. There was a spastic search for entertainment. Previously we had tranquil dances to the crackling sound of the gramophone, sober family get-togethers with bingo games ("tombola), and other fun and traditional pastimes.

Now, instead, there were unrestrained dances to the music of improvised orchestras. No longer were there timid approaches to the languid, mellow notes of the tango. Instead the ladies were catapulted high up in the air, always higher. This was the new dance that was all the range, the boogie woogie, the dance of the moment.

Young kids pirouetted in fearless acrobatics, jumps, flights in the air, landings that were hardly harmonious or elegant, unashamed exhibitions of parts of the body once demurely concealed. More than happy girls having fun they seemed like tarantula spiders.

The Italian language was enriched with foreign words that few understood and too many people used. Etiquette was massacred.

Rules became impositions against a much desired liberation that was won with such difficulty. Liberation - this word was used to one's ease and liking, it became a word so elastic that each person used it for their own purpose and consumption.

This sudden new way of life made a deep impression on me. I began to have some doubt in the mental wellness of my parents. All their teachings became nullified, my good upbringing didn't exist anymore. I heard the placid voice of Mamma, 'Piera you are a girl, not a wild boy, one does not chew with one's mouth open, you must keep good manners,' and a thousand exhortations and directions that make a person a civil being.

THE VILLA OF THE COUNTESS

American chewing gum arrived, a great achievement of liberation of course, the mouth open, a continual mashing of teeth, the pleasure of moving around a kind of disgusting sticky ball from one tooth to the other. Important discussions were treated like pingpong rackets, one word and the little ball of gum flew to the right, another word and naturally, visibly, it flew back to the left. Then when it had lost any flavor and you wanted to get rid of it you stuck it wherever you wanted.

Drinking glasses weren't used any more and it didn't matter that they were more hygenic and simpler to use. Using drinking glasses was an imposition, meanwhile clinging to a glass bottle represented free choice, an unequivocal sign of liberty.

Mamma expressed her worry that Attico and I would be taken with all this urge for novel entertainment. By now we were at a risky impressionable age, longing to know, see, and feel ourselves as grown ups.

This danger was real and thus Mamma decided to move us again, a few kilometers from Bertinoro. Echoes of the wild life in town would reach us in a much more muted way from far away.

The Countess Acquaderni, a friend of Mamma's, put at our disposal a part of her villa. It had been an ancient convent that had become a summer house, with antique frescoed walls, imposing halls, infinitely long corridors. At every step, lives already lived were evoked once again, tragedies never told, desperations, mystic forces and gratifying happinesses.

We acclimated ourselves to the new house, but not to the two white statues, as tall as real people, that ruled on either side of the great staircase. They scared me terribly. Even today I struggle to remember well what that staircase was like, due to the great speed with which I was able to sweep up it to arrive home, panting and amazed to have made it past the statues.

Forlimpopoli and Forlì were closer than Bertinoro to the new house but the fun of the trip remained intact. We would still go to Bertinoro and half way there were greeted by festive cries.

Near the villa was a big farmhouse where we were welcomed jovially as friends. Attico had become friends with Alvaro, the young son of the farmer. A simple and loyal boy, Alvaro was always in love with our other friend Marisa. He was constantly in an uncertain search for a mechanism to make her capitulate.

The restless urge for freedom and progress had not yet contaminated their healthy and traditional life. The grandfather and grandmother were the support pillar of a serene and respectful community. The father, greatly disabled by war with a wooden leg, evoked in me the image of famous pirates from novels. His warm and calm look, however, did not render the comparison.

I remember the gatherings in the spacious kitchen, the fireplace crackling. The grandmother with practically sacred movements kneaded the piadina dough, fragrant disks that filled the air with odors never smelled again, the movements repeated for centuries and never the same.

The piadina, a little circle of dough shaped by expert hands, was eased down onto a red-hot grill. The bread was perforated with a fork, then turned upside down to bake in a ritual created by the hands of the marvelous women of Emilia Romagna.

As soon as it was cooked it was placed on the pastry board, hot and fragrant, and divided with precise mastery into four slices that formed a bastion of savory goodness. Then came the sweet Albana wine, a golden liquid that was sipped slowly. We children had to settle only for the fragrance of the wine, it was the ideal finishing touch to that delicious piadina.

I got to know other girls my age. Ave, tall with dark hair, already big for her age, responsible, and always behind the counter of her parents' little grocery shop. Kind and affectionate, she would wait restlessly for visits by Marisa and me. Ave lived to hear us recount our adventures, our dreams. In doing so she could escape her world that was too small, and become once again a young lady.

Marisa was not very tall but already lovely, more woman than child. She lived in a farmhouse not far from Bisciara, that was the name of the little village. Her upturned nose, her cheekbones gently accented and brightened with adorable freckles, her pleasing laugh all were the eternal unfulfilled dream of Alvaro.

Fast runs through the country fields, cherry trees with branches overloaded with succulent fruit, perfumed mulberry trees, we were wide-eyed for a world we had yet to discover.

After school I would go to her house, along a narrow path, long rows of vines held up by mulberry trees, a blooming and generous land. I would open the front door calling out to her with a big voice. While I waited I observed the massive entryway. From one side reigned a portrait of Stalin, his thick mustache and low forehead. From the other hung the image of Jesus who held in his hand his flaming red heart with a halo of a thousand shining rays of light.

Two images seemingly at odds but instead compatible. Stalin represented the redemption of the political dream, Jesus the respect for God.

Marisa's wish was to go to the park at Villa Prati. The park was gloomily known for the murder of two young German soldiers who just minutes before being barbariously murdered had toasted a drink with their assassins.

Hundred year old trees, silent witnesses of criminal acts, rose towards the sky. It was a place of charm and mystery that evoked an unknown world to our simple lives. We ventured into the thick of the trees, paths that were merely suggestions. Moss in a thousand colors enveloped the trunks; dark and compact it came to life at the touch of my hand.

Peeking out from behind a dense bush, we had a dreamy panorama presented before us. A little lake crossed by a fragile bridge. And thus we violated the solitary walks of the young Count Cosimo. Tall and dressed in white, he went along with a sad aura towards the bridge, his gaze lost in the crystalline waters of the stream. Without expressing any emotion, he seemed alien and immune to the serene beauty around us.

Slowly he would resume his walk back into the thickness of the forest. Unbeknownst to him, he had become our Prince Charming. We dreamt of impossible loves and adventurous elopements. The fact that the Count was one and we were two, and that he was unaware of our presence and our fantasies, in no way constituted any obstacles.

The joy of unknown feelings, yearnings and dreams not yet experienced. Cosimo, so sad and unaware, lost in his own thoughts. It was for us the first feeling of butterflies in our stomachs, the seeds of a childhood that was fading away, the mystery of the future behind the corner.

We had happy years there, evenings celebrated in many different kitchens, a happy racket made by simple people. Anecdotes and memories of the war. There were solemn remembrances of those who were no longer with us, and the tone of voice would lower to a painful whisper.

Such peace, finally. The intense perfume of the piadina cooked continuously, the Albana wine nursed between one word and another. Attico and I felt at home even though we were not one of them, we wanted to safeguard like a treasure those feelings until the end. While you are living them you know that they will always be in you, a shelter and oasis of peace in a world you no longer understand.

The first elections came. The winners were the hammer and sickle[12] and the crossed shield. Normality tried to take the upper hand on total anarchy masked as freedom. Remnants of the Anglo Americans were all the rage, the Italian language was notably bastardized. Our musical "sì va bene" became "ok", metallic and terse, a little exclamation that meant everything and nothing. It indicated either approval, evasive verification, or mysterious response. You could choose which one you wanted, it was a way to avoid going deeper in conversation.

The days passed in waiting for some kind of news. We were immigrants into our own country and the turning point arrived with various reactions. Mamma and Franco were clearly thrilled, Brunella was enthusiastic, but Attico and I were more perplexed than overjoyed.

We were to depart again. This time we were headed towards Rome, a town called Rocca di Papa, a new life had been organized for us in under an hour.

We would have liked to stay in Bertinoro, for we felt like an integral part of the community there. It was our home, we were no longer closed in the family cocoon. We had started to disentangle the delicate thread of silk of childhood security, and the spiral that we glimpsed was very enticing and rich in a thousand expectations.

We had said goodbye to RhodesRhodes, mythical and irrecoverable.

Now goodbye to Bertinoro, tall and gracious.

And then of course, would come the last Goodbye. Goodbye Rocca di Papa, goodbye...Goodbye even to you.

1950: ARRIVAL IN SARDINIA

"Memories are the only part of our sacred and inalienable life, beyond all the human occurrences, that escape the dominion of destiny.
They cannot be changed or be taken from us, possession of them is eternal and unchangeable."

-Seneca

Slowly the azure sea rose to meet us, and here we were at our new destinazione, Sardinia.

Glimpses of barren landscapes began to appear. My anguish tried desperately to find some excuse to make the nostalgia less painful. I was suffocated with grief, my tears obscured the hostile land in front of me that I did not want or like.

A frantic bounce of pride and the airplane touched down. A shout of joy flew through the air, a shout made not of joy but of freedom, to cover the various jerks, creaks, and suspicious sounds.

The old airplane with some decorum came to a stop. We got off silently. The only ones to reveal a certain enthusiasm were Franco's two little birds. They beat their wings frantically between rapturous chirping. Franco looked at them and being the most practical and rational being I have ever known, pronounced, "They're hungry."

Attico, a perfectionist, examined the underbelly of the aircraft. He wanted to see the reason for those sinister sounds and squeaks that had livened up our journey.

Mamma and Papà were quiet.

There before us was the sea. We were on an island, hoping to relive the dream of Rhodes. I looked around me with fierce skepticism, and saw only long rows of eucalyptus, a landscape spare and arid. I had never seen anything so ugly.

Mamma approached, at first I thought she wanted to console me since my dismay was so apparent.

"Piera, do you mind giving me your flat shoes? My feet are swollen."

I looked at her incredulously. Up until that moment heels were an absolute taboo for me. Anytime I had asked her, she immediately responded, 'You are still too young.'

We swapped shoes and with an unsure step, wobbling along, I was off to conquer Sardinia. Not without difficulty I climbed onto the bus. All of my attention was fixated on the astounding event that in such a short time I had become a grownup.

A line of asphalt that was the road wound between ancient olive groves and brambles of prickly pear. The wind in the olive branches adorned them with a reflective silver. Some little houses came into view, one against the other, almost to protect each other.

Small windows modestly closed, doors held just even so slightly ajar to see the new arrivals - us.

We arrived in a large open space. I was feeling a desolation that is not possible to imagine. There were piles of rubble everywhere, and the walls that made up the perimeter of the piazza were, to say the least, tragically grotesque. One part pink, the other white, I realized that those walls were a string of rooms of collapsed houses.

And so we learned that recently there had been a terrible flood. The signs it left behind were more than evident, the tragedy was still very apparent. From the prickly pear bushes hung every sort of object - shoes, rags. It seemed that a maleficent monster had wanted to add a note of spectacular tragedy to the already ghostly landscape.

Leaves torn to pieces displayed an out of place milky whiteness. Objects and rags moved in the breeze in a sinister harmony of embellishments. There was a great display of death and desolation. Mud and water had swept through everything without pity. Houses, symbols of peace and serenity, had been transformed into cages of death. So many dead, so many children and adults flattened by mud against ceilings, entire families wiped out by an inexorable tide which had slammed directly onto the pond at Elmas.

I forgot that I was a grown up, I forgot the heels I was wearing. I lost my last crumbs of dignity and began to cry inconsolably. We walked towards the house that would be ours for a few days while we waited for the other house that Papà had rented for us to free up.

We saw our temporary house down the road from afar. It was set between many other small houses and unlike them, had two floors. It held court pompously and was fully aware of being the symbol of well to do success, like someone who was better off than many others. It had a balcony and a white facade with windows outlined in a darker color.

On one side of our house were the shorter houses that seemed almost proud to be near ours. On the other side, a street opened up to the Church. It was called Via dell'Arma Azzurra, Street of the Blue Armed Forces, a street that called to mind infinite spaces, silver meteors that streaked across the heavens, intrepid men in glorious sky blue uniforms - the world of my childhood.

The houses made up long, tall rows of cement lining the streets. In the center of each house was a large front door, where stains of green dust tried to peep through the wall. There were oleanders, pale flowers, mortified for having dared to bloom. One sensed, rather than saw that they were inhabited.

I paused, hearing the agitated murmur of my parents and sensing the illusion of a new Rhodes disappearing. Raising my eyes I saw an unpaved road, long and sundrenched, hostile. Doors opening just slightly ajar seeped with curiosity and a hardly veiled antipathy that asked, "Where do these people come from? What do they want with our town?"

The furious and rhythmic slamming of the doors was pure rejection of something that they didn't want to know - the outside world. It was in defense of their way of life, their ancestral misery of always having been considered last.

When we arrived at our house, we rested the luggage on a veranda which was more like a type of hut promoted for the occasion to be a veranda. Franco opened his box with the little birds and stroked them slowly, apparently unaware of everything that was going on around him. Brunella was oblivious of the confusion. Her world was still Mamma and Papà and us, her gaze attracted to the cows that pastured nearby.

We had left behind the cows of Rocca di Papa, and here were different cows. But the disagreeable stink that they emitted was still the same. Attico was engrossed in studying small bundled figures intent on watering the garden. They bowed, they rose again and moved with the hoe the modest embankments in the ground to irrigate first one groove, then the other, with a constant and precise rhythm.

In the distance was a dam, a work constructed far too late. With its imposing presence it embittered all the survivors of the flood's devastating handiwork, practically a prank monument erected but overdue.

A row of eucalyptus trees, their leaves changed to a silvery green at every breath of the wind, seemed to unleash a hopeful music.

I tried to find anything beautiful in that bare landscape, my mind started interposing on top of it beautiful places from my childhood, the variegated green of the forest and the far away glitter of Lake Albano, or the purplish roses and cascades of bougainville from Rhodes.

This stirred memories of my friends from Rocca di Papa...I saw again the frantic look on my friend Renzo's face, "Piera, don't go," his gaze lost in possibilities never redeemed, dreams shattered amid the clattering of the train. Long letters from Patrizio, full of heart breaking nostalgia. "Piera, don't go". The tears of my girlfriends, Bianca, Marisa, their words of encouragement, "You'll be back, we will take these same walks to the Madonna del Tufo, we will dream of the husbands we would like to meet...little by little by little cherishing these memories, we will wait for you!"

A scream cut through the air, sending into fragments my fortress of remembrances and nostalgic dreams. I opened my eyes and saw Mamma planted flat, just fifty meters from the fake veranda. The tragic nature of the moment was underlined by her bare feet, because without shoes she was not even able to stay upright. I tried to imagine what dramatic and absurd thing had caused this. Perhaps a cow had crossed over onto our veranda?

No, the cows were all there in place nibbling the grass calmly, kept under the control of Nadi the dog. Unaware of the tragedy in progress, they focused all their attention on eating grass and also the arduous task of whipping away with their tails the flies dedicated to molest and assault these placid beasts.

I looked at Mamma, her face lined with darkest terror. Attico was lining up little sticks, creating a fence that seemed to have no sense. Papà continued to read. Franco was pushing ants around here and there, making them go back to their house. To the ants Franco's robust logic didn't make sense. They wanted to stay where they were or go where they had decided to go.

I was puzzled. What tragic event had caused Mamma's distress? Mamma's hand pointed toward the roof. With an expression of fear enhanced with a grimace of total disgust, she slowly raised her eyes upwards. I saw the beamed roof that held up layers of straw. And there a type of lizard passed along, indifferent to her terror. It stopped, then threw itself with lightning quick precision onto its buzzing prey, a fly, only to restart the hunt once again immediately afterward.

Dressed for vital security, the lizard wandered shamelessly, camouflaged, aware of her chameleon-like powers.

"Mamma!" Franco now came near with his rebellious locks of hair, eyes as penetrating as needles, "We can't kill her, she eats the mosquitoes."

This was completely iron solid logic to him but not to Mamma, who refused categorically to reenter the house. In an authoritarian voice, but with an imploring tone, she said, "Quinzio, kill that serpent." For Mamma, all animals close to the ground were serpents.

Papà got up slowly, hands on his sides. His hair refused to cover his bald head. By now his hair had been degraded to a simple flap covering, and it rose up more warlike than ever given the moment. He resembled the cartoon character Sor Pampurio.[13]

And thus Papà began his strategy of attack. With slow and cautious movements he studied the position of the hungry gecko, who did not know it had been promoted to serpent.

Papà commenced a thorough analysis of the enemy. He had to choose with what object he would strike it - a shoe? A stick? But they were weapons too imprecise, and they increased the likelihood of escape.

The decision was pained and difficult, keeping in consideration that to trick Mamma would be difficult - only the corpse of the animal would prove for sure its death.

Papà got up on a chair, and he was completely ready. But in the meantime, the sated gecko was no longer there, the hunt was over. We hoped for the future in Mamma's myopia and in knowing that geckos have a complete aversion for humans.

ADAPTING TO A NEW LAND

Days of idleness as we waited that the real house would free up and that the furniture would arrive.

We began to examine the world that surrounded us. The list of negatives outnumbered greatly the positives. We began to make our first introductions, not to the locals, but to people like us, exiles from the Italian mainland, colleagues of Papà along with their wives and children.

In the afternoons, in the sultry stillness of that summer, there were long games of cards. Canasta was all the rage, but my parents preferred briscola, scopa, and 'three sevens with the death'. But the most frequently played game was rummy.

I didn't play. Outside, near the house was a large basin for washing vegetables. Seated on the edge I surrendered myself to my world of fantasy, avoiding a reality that I liked less and less.

A few passersby slowed their steps, their curiosity in me made me close myself even more into my imaginary world. With my bare arms, my blonde hair, my solemn and slightly swaying gait, they had already labeled me a brazen continental Italian.

I attempted a shy overture of friendship with the girls who worked in the vegetable gardens. In the evening they would gather around the large basin to wash the vegetables. Shapeless forms, they seemed embarrassed by their own feminine beauty. With each passerby they hid their face behind a scarf. Even their hands were covered by clothing. They moved the heads of lettuce in the water with a monotonous and mechanical rhythm. They never looked me in the eye, a poorly concealed act of rebellion for being so different from me.

I remember one of the girls in particular, Barbanina, who sat during lunch trying to find shade that was parsimoniously cast on the wall of the basin. A head of crispy lettuce in her hand, her teeth sank into the fragrant leaves. I smelled the perfume of the marvelous Sardinian bread and perhaps I even envied her the life she had - so pure, simple, and true.

One day I was finally accepted. She pulled her scarf away a little and unveiled an unexpected and cheerful beauty, a smile full of joy, a purity without equal. Those white teeth that dived into the succulent pulp of tomatoes with a palpable and primordial pleasure. Little beads of purply juice rolled down her face. Her calloused hand wiped away the drops in absolute gratification and total contentment, thanksgiving and devotion to life whatever it might be.

She held pride in being part of her land, a little sliver of granite in a territory never conquered, never humiliated, never dominated. And there on the edge of that basin, I too, wanted to be a little sliver of granite. I wanted to have a pride of belonging, a sensation of having arrived, of no longer feeling an exile in my own country.

Winning over the place was simpler than getting used to it. It was as if progress had stopped fifty years prior. For the continental Italians, the island of Sardinia was a land of penance, of punishment and ransom. Anyone on the continent who had sullied oneself with a crime was sent to the penal colonies on the island. For political crimes, the sea and the distance were excellent deterrents. Sardinia helped cool off boiling spirits.

And so out of this was born the Sardinians' belief that the continental Italians were delinquents, and that it was better to not have anything to do with them. Italy was absent, very far away, but even so the Sardinians still felt profoundly Italian.

How many Sardinian soldiers lie under Italian soil? How many rushed to the extreme sacrifice of their lives, to defend a land that had ignored and marginalized them? Heroic pages forgotten, bravery worn down in a sublime offering for a continental land so far away, a continental land with a tendency to neglect and forget.

I began to love Sardinia. It was a land of contradictions, of honor and traditions. It was a land of a thousand facets, concealed sentiments, friendships difficult to win but once won, eternal and indissoluble.

Progress went forward very slowly. The Sardinians respected with willful determination their customs and dress. You had to adjust your step to that of a tenacious people deeply proud of their traditions and their history.

If they accepted unbridled progress they would have to change their traditions and their customs. And thus, every new thing became nursed slowly, measured even if it were actually desired, with a respectful surrender in regard to customs and dress.

I had come from a different reality in terms of progress. Rocca di Papa was near Rome and had absorbed that city's comparative tendency for progress. Indeed, rampant progress was frittered away as if it were the only means of survival. Progress had made Rome a cosmopolitan city, open to every invasion. It survived because of its glorious history, rendering it unique and distinctive. Every little fragment of rock, every monument, every column that rose illustriously towards the sky bore witness of a power of glory and history for all the land. As long as even one of these witnesses endured with respect, Rome would live divine and eternal.

Sardinia took possession of me. It was an unparalleled world there for us to discover. Lofty values and true sentiments, respect and honor were all fused to forge the Sardinian people. Women were mythic in their appearance. Their lowered eyes and harmonious movements hid a sheer will, an iron tenaciousness.

And so despite my moments of nostalgia, my regret for everything I had left behind, the green of the forests, the starry sky that seemed to dive into the dark Albano lake...all of that was a little farther away now. I became interested to learn about this new land I didn't know, and this filled me with a curious expectation.

I didn't have any more tears but a sweet awareness that tomorrow would be a new day. And so we entered into daily Sardinian life, a life which we would share for many years. We wanted to find out what were the positives of this world that was hostile to us, we wanted to become a part of it.

I wanted to make even the noises mine. The creaking of the old carriage, the barking of a dog seeking someone to communicate with, the long whistle of the train, the lowing of the cattle who were always vainly attempting to rebel against the dictatorial command of the magnificent dog Nadi, who tried to divert them towards a different pasture.

In the distance a light sound of a small trumpet shook the silence. The town crier announced the latest news. His legs were crossed, standing, for a more stable balance, as he was rather old. His body was stuffed into an old uniform, a remnant of the First World War, evidenced by the long bands that covered his calves as if they were boots.

With a shrill voice he announced the slaughter of a sheep and the subsequent sale of the meat. The front doors opened slowly and chatter bounced from one house to another, anticipating the unexpected change to the usual daily menu.

I wanted to be a Sardinian woman. I wanted it with all my might.

But to start by eating the meat of a sheep seemed excessive to me. I would remain, despite myself, a lousy, continental Italian.

CAGLIARI

I used to take the train from the little station of Elmas to the huge old market in Cagliari, which was mostly a fish market. The train would arrive from Olbia, which is on the other side of Sardinia. These were old locomotives fed with coal, in a continuous voyage between north and south. Worn out wooden seats of a pale color maintained by the constant passage of the passengers.

The rest of the train was all black, the windows dark with soot preserved many fingerprints. The transparency of the glass was a feature that had been lost in time. The floor was sanitized and shined with abundant buckets of naphtha oil that served the purpose of, other than killing microbes, keeping passengers agile. The passengers employed acrobatic exertions to stay on their feet without slipping, and then landed on the seats, dusting them off.

The trip was brief. After just a few kilometers one arrived at the station in Cagliari. Everything here too was black, the platforms, sidewalks and buildings. From the color of the face of the passengers, darker or lighter, one could hypothesize as to how long their stay on board the train had been.

A coming and going of people in a jagged medley of colors. Women in their colorful dresses, graceful in their movements. Their wide skirts seemed to rise and fall in the breeze, too lovely to touch the ground, and they had little corsets that outlined the fullness of their breasts.

Faces framed by elaborate lace highlighted limitless beauty, while little bonnets held back cascades of silky raven black hair.

They had a slow and regal gait, deep and velvety eyes. Their glances could almost be described as timid, but more accurately said held a calm and absolute awareness of the real pride of the Sardinian woman.

Via Roma led away from one end of the port, with its thousands of continuous and frenetic activities. Flights of seagulls brushed the sea and then rose again toward the sky, only to then swoop back again into a dive towards the water, connecting those two blues - the sky and the sea - with their white and silver arabesque flights.

The arched porticoes weaved pleasantly along the streets, sometimes balanced and sometimes contrasting, symbols of civilizations from long ago. Ancient invasions, thousands of comings and goings of people who left behind unerasable traces.

The white palace of the town hall tried to soften the blue of the sea and the sky with its blinding whiteness. Century old trees formed a divider between the Via Roma street and the sea. The water played an infinite game of bowing and rising, and little umbrellas seemed to dance in the air.

Largo San Felice was a lovely climb, at the top it finished in a piazza that had a statue in the center. On the left was the church of Sant'Anna, and on the right the elegant Via Manno. And a little further up, the market, which was my destination. As ancient as it was historic, the market was a civilized clamoring, a refined way of speaking, a continuous flowing in and out of people. And there, there was progress.

Fresh fish still flopping about peeped out of the stands, as well as a profusion of a thousand products of the highest quality. A very selective clientele with obvious economic power browsed the stalls. I found my coveted cutlets and retraced my steps, looking around as I went.

Cagliari, a thousand times invaded, a thousand times conquered by foreign peoples. Its palaces contained the stamp of so many civilizations, different styles which were witness to various progressions. Every angle was a treasure to discover with scrupulous reverence.

Cagliari, whole and uncontaminated, encapsulated the indelible mark of the Sardinian culture.

I returned home with my cutlets, the reminder reward and chore. I looked at the vegetable tub, where the lettuce floated, moved around by Barberina's expert hands. Tomorrow she would hang them at the stall of the market, but in that moment they seemed like floating flowers.

It was strange, Rocca di Papa now felt light years away. Here the little noises, the houses, they seemed to me nests of peace. The rustling of the eucalyptus trees said to me, "you are home, you are home."

SARDINIA - THE TIDAL POOL

Attico had met some boys his age. Since we were still not accepted by the locals, our friends were families like us who had come from the continent. One of those families were the Snidersigs. The father was an exile of his hometown of Istria, sick with regret and nostalgia but above all full of impotent rage. His wife was a sweet and gentle woman, full of love for her family. Evelina, calm and chubby child, was the sweet playmate of Brunella. Elio was the same age of Franco. And then there was Enzo, surely the prototype of a boy who even today would make all the girls go crazy.

Tall and blonde, with a gladiator's physique and a sincere smile, he was captivating. He was just a little bit younger than me and immediately he took on the difficult task of protecting me. Or better said, flanking Attico in that task, as it was Attico's main job since the day of my birth.

We started going to the sea together. Really it was a tidal pool fed by the sea, but all the same it was a tidal pool. Swampy plants and rushes grew there, and little coves jaggedly cut the shore. On the other side of the tidal pool were modest houses shielded on the high barren cliff. There I would watch unimaginably beautiful sunsets, waterfalls of fire that seemed to challenge nature. The tidal pool seemed to burn in a thousand purple showers, almost liquefying in the red flame of the sun.

The little coves were outlined by incredible beaches of rocks, not sand. Stretches of seashells, large and small in marvelous shapes and in a thousand shades of white, recalled the poetry of the sea and offered a cheerful harmony for the eyes. But it was completely another sensation to walk on top of them, for your poor feet it was an undertaking for the stoic, comparable only to tortures inflicted on the worst sinners.

When you walked there, it was so difficult that any composed gait became a dance of absurd silliness. We lowered our eyes to make out the sporadic and tiny spots that were less cutting and pointy. But regardless of all the pain to our extremities, that was the most carefree and happy period of my life. Childhood was behind me and the future all to discover.

The landing strip of the Elmas airport bordered the tidal pool, and only a simple metal fence divided the two zones. Every now and then a sign warned "Military Zone, No Entry". Airplanes glistened under the sun in all of their magnificence. Their engines rumbled, propellers cutting the air to push them onward towards limitless space. Like seagulls without souls, they defied the immensity of the skies.

The tidal pool was there. The water wasn't crystal clear, but the muddy bottom didn't stop us from seeing it as the most beautiful place in the world. I learned to swim under the watchful and careful guidance of Enzo, who had lived for several years in Taranto by the sea. Water was his natural element and he was a perfect swimmer. His assured and athletic presence conquered my fear of the water and I convinced myself I had become a mermaid.

The days flew by peacefully, full of attempts to triumph over the prickly seashells, telling stories about our short lives so far, and dreams for the future. With my gaze I tried to follow the fearless maneuvers of the seagulls. They skimmed over the water and then rose again clasping their agonized prey, thrashing mullets that tried with final jerks to achieve an improbable escape.

The tidal pool was almost always calm, but continually livened up by the leaps and routines of the mullets who leaped in silvery flights. For them it was a game, for the seagulls it was survival.

HOW I SCANDALIZED THE SARDINIANS

One morning as we arrived, we found the little beach strangely crowded. We couldn't see a glimpse of any living being, just a series of improvisatory tents. We thought it was a friendly gathering. We stopped, a little worried, at the edge of the beach. Nothing. Absolute silence. With apprehension and curiosity we approached the picturesque camp. We set up like on all the other days, our regular daily ritual, towels stretched out under the sun, with us sitting above them to keep them from flying away.

Slowly the edges of the tents lifted. Sardinian women appeared, suddenly becoming animated with curious looks, consternation and dismay. Voices whispered in the Sardinian language, and the only thing we could understand was "tittia ta ddanu", or "How cold they must be! What a mess!"

The more elderly women accompanied the exclamations with repeated signs of the cross. Very concerned, we took a collective examination of our situation. Our bathing suits were placed in the right positions, nothing seemed to us so serious as to justify such an attack.

Reassured, I began to take off my dress. Little by little the beach became animated again. All their eyes were focused on me. It turned out I was the cause of all this agitation with my shameless, indecent, and obscene nudity.

I was wearing a white two piece with little red acorns, the bottom was rigorously modest, the top had a task that was purely theoretical, seeing as my chest had nothing to hold up. I was flat, pathetically flat.

Unfortunately, from that moment on I became the symbol of continental Italian women, brazen and lost. And it got worse. I ascended true honors during Sunday mass in the priest's homily. He warned the young women that they were absolutely banned from imitating the depraved foreigner (me) who had undermined the traditional country dress with her obscene nudity.

This episode raised quite a racket. There was even a journalist, who, short on any real news, felt it his duty to document the scandal in person. It was a short article, outlining simply that a practically nude blond continental Italian was wagging her hips languidly on a carpet of seashells.

Previous to this, I was just starting to become accepted as normal. But this episode notably slowed the process of entering a community skeptical of natural declivity.

I decided to not return to the tidal pool for a few days, at least until the fuss had died down a bit. Instead, from home, I began managing our family correspondence from the continent. These were letters received with total joy, no longer with tears but a peaceful delight.

My responses to our relatives on the continent omitted all that was not positive, while everything that I had begun to love and understand was exaggerated.

AND LIFE GOES ON

The day arrived to leave our temporary house and enter our real one, since our furniture had arrived. My tiny world began to take more shape. In the new house, only one room had a ceiling of straw, so mama's fear of the hungry lizards was reduced and held at bay. Also, her myopia prevented her from seeing them on the colored walls. Their nudity and transparency were their defense, since they managed to camouflage themselves to the same color of the walls. And for the sake of our own tranquility we kept their secrets.

I was sharing fully my life with that of Attico, and I considered all the boys like buddies, friends, or another type of brother.

In those days Enzo was really all that I wanted. From him, I had learned to swim and to cross the waters' flow without any fear, sensing his constant and safe protection. We would gather bunches of heather in the country, the wind in my hair. I had all my life all in front of me.

Attico came home one day from the tidal pool with a euphoric exuberance. He had met another new boy who was a terrific swimmer and spoke of him with deep admiration. He tried to intrigue me seeing as how I was in a phase of imprecise interests. I was a bit bored, a bit impatient for new expectations that seemed late to arrive.

One morning I decided to return to the tidal pool. Attico and Franco had already gone ahead. I arrived unexpectedly and was welcomed by everyone with a shout of joy. Attico, smiling, introduced me to his new friend.

"Piera, this is Gregorio. Gregorio, this is my sister"

With a slight bow, Gregorio clasped my hand. His gallantry floored me completely. To do a little bow and to take my hand were things practically unheard of between us kids. Intrigued, I looked at him from head to toe, meeting a gaze between glacial and sarcastic.

He waited for me to sit down before taking up again his supine position next to Attico, and completely forgetting my presence. Every now and then he sat up, without a word, his gaze lost in the distance. He held his cigarette tightly between his thumb and index finger, his attention focused on the spirals of smoke and on his attempt to reduce the cigarette butt to the smallest possible stub. I was smitten.

Other than his initial greeting, he treated my presence with absolute indifference, and my passion suffered a blow. Slyly, I looked at him. An athletic physique, wide shoulders, and narrow hips. He moved elegantly and naturally. He wasn't bad. My feminine pride consoled itself by saying that he was old and that he had a mustache. I loathed men with mustaches.

I focused on the flights of the striped mullets, completely ignoring Gregorio in my turn. After his solitary swim, he dried every drop of water with just a few movements, carefully refolding the towel and putting it back in his bag as if it were a precious object. His motions were slow and precise, as if he were savoring something from a forgotten time.

Then with a "Ciao, see you tomorrow", he mounted a strange vehicle that previously would have been called a bicycle but was now just a jumble of old pieces of metal. These pieces seemed to be fighting against each other, protesting in disagreement at the motions with a constant and prolonged creaking.

I sat up to fully enjoy the spectacle of his bicycle maneuvers. He skirted the metal fence at an unnecessary speed, arrogant and disagreeable, full of himself.

I looked at Attico and asked, "Is he always like that?"

Smiling, Attico responded, "Sometimes he is even worse."

THE BOYS AT THE TIDAL POOL

Gregorio was very different from Attico's other friends. A persisting curiosity buzzed inside me, but every timid overture I made shipwrecked into a sea of absolute indifference. It almost seemed that my presence annoyed him. Resigned, I dedicated my time to the rest of the group. Enzo was always smiling and available, steadfast and handsome. He resembled a Riace bronze, which in those days hadn't even been discovered. I took long swims under Enzo's constant protection.

A new boy from town joined our group. Piero, dark haired and well built. With deep velvety eyes, he began to court me calmly. Kind, almost submissive, he would give me little attentions here and there, furtive glances of admiration. People noticed because Piero already had been in love with another girl, Marisa. They began to speak about their great contrasting love - he from a rich, land-owning family, and Marisa from a very modest family. Their love was born practically in infancy and developed despite the insurmountable contrasts and bans of social class that were typical in that period.

For my part, aside from the novelty of it, it represented the concept of "the nail hammers out the other nail." (When there is a nail embedded in wood, the best way to remove that nail is by hammering another nail into it...) Piero seemed to have given up on his impossible love and was trying to chase thoughts of Marisa away by focusing on me.

I considered Piero a good friend, but he had mistaken my exuberant, comradely and extraordinary friendliness for interest. Or at least for possible future interest. I thought of him as an affectionate and kind friend, and he makes up a part of my happiest memories.

But Sardinia in those years was a complexity of rules, honor, and traditions. And thus, without any encouragement from my part, a classic proposal of marriage arrived.

The messenger of this proposal was Francesco, friendly and honest, with a decisive and determined nature. I must digress a moment, to mention Francesco's own very similar story. Francesco had been a rich landowner, but had purposefully thrown away his very substantial patrimony while waiting for a separation from his wife. Perhaps he had done this to avoid paying alimony, or perhaps to demolish the social position which did not permit him to live with his great love, Francesca. She was dependent on his gilded world, but too far removed by social standards.

Francesco's profound love had bridged every gap, and his affection, the real kind, had eliminated every obstacle between him and Francesca. Francesco now had a life without money but was serene, he had a real and palpable happiness with Francesca.

Self-restrained and serious, Francesco was the one who conveyed to me Piero's request.

I listened incredulously. Nothing in Piero's behavior had foretold such a grandiose request. I thought for a moment that it might be a joke, but Francesco's gravitas led me to shed this hypothesis.

When I recovered from my shock I protested, saying, "But Piero is my friend and he deeply loves Marisa, sooner or later they will achieve their dream together'. I thought of Marisa with her cascade of blonde curls, and her indomitable determination to want to live her love story with Piero. I listened to Francesco with remorseful reverence given such a solemn moment. The request was precise and indisputably clear. I tried to smile as I considered what possible response I could give, a response that would be meaningful and also unappealable.

"I'm sorry, Francesco, but I am already in love with someone else."

The liberating smile on Francesco's face helped me understand that he, the messenger, was not in agreement that Piero should ask my hand in marriage. Francesco knew that Piero and Marisa, instead, were meant to be.

I began to wait for Attico's new friend in the mornings at the tidal pool with a bit too much and too obvious anticipation.

Gregorio was ever more disagreeable and brusque. When I would see him appear in the distance, brushing the metal fence with reckless acrobatics, I wished that he would fall. I wanted to see in him some sign of human weakness, to shake that glacial self-confidence, his gaze lost in unknown faraway places, his way of making us feel childish and infantile.

With my face hidden in my arms I followed his every move, his way of being. He was meticulous and always the same. It was as if he had to relearn things that were gone and forgotten, to reclaim himself from the day to day. I had acquired the art of re-vealing that I was seeing nothing.

His physique was statuesque, he was a boy but already a man too. His nostalgia was always more evanescent and far away. Despite my best intentions to resist, an exciting and unknown sentiment grew inside me. My hopes would die and then be re-born at a supersonic speed.

There were dark days and then days of euphoric exaltation. Slowly, very slowly, I began to get to know him better, helped along by what I heard from Attico. I sometimes saw his eyes catch fire with light, a thousand golden flecks. They were no longer always gloomy. I felt the heat of his gaze. I respected what

I now could recognize as his shy and fearful interest in me. I wanted to know him better, to his core.

Gregorio was a political refugee, a soldier of the so-called wrong side. He fled from a cruel hunt for the defeated. Now far from his own lands he sought the answers to a thousand Why's.

Gregorio was often closed off, so enigmatic to me. I was drawn to him and ever more curious about him. I began to give a real significance to every one of his odd gestures. His methodic fervor in completing otherwise normal actions was for him a reclaiming of life, a life that he had previously lost hope to have. He wanted to feel miraculously alive, he wanted to forget the terrible memories of friends killed at his side, in their desperate shout "Long live Italy!"

He felt it was his fault to still be alive while they had died, to feel the heat of the sun while they couldn't. He lightly brushed against me with his gaze, shyly, as if even I might disappear suddenly.

Admiration, tenderness, attraction, his glance would animate suddenly in those thousand golden flecks. The boy thirsty for love and for life took over, his eyes lost in mine, his hand clasping mine, a glimmer of hope.

But around the corner even more atrocious battles awaited. But this will be another story, just mine and Gregorio's, a love sixty years long and that will last beyond this life. And so day by day he had me enter into his life and I became an integral part of it. I knew his world of a thousand light years ago, so far from mine.

I convinced myself that love can conquer any distances and can level out any difficulties. Too soon I would understand that this is not always true.

Little by little, I entered into his past. Aloof phrases, tormented pauses, hiccups held for a time that would never return. A world lived with joy and recalled with helpless anguish.

GREGORIO'S CHILDHOOD

"I don't let a single phantom memory fade with the clouds, and it is my perennial awareness of the past that sometimes causes my pain, but if I had to choose between joy and pain, I wouldn't trade the pains of my heart with the joys of the whole world ... "
-    K. Gibran

She had already vanished, elegant not beautiful, the elegance of innate distinction. At the door she had given him a little gesture goodbye, distracted and rushed. He followed her with his gaze while he touched his hair with his little hand. He could almost still feel the heat of his mother's hand which had rested there for just a moment. His governess squeezed his hand, to reassure him that she was still there. "You'll see, tomorrow your mother will play with you, and in a few days your papà will return. Stay strong!"

His childhood was sprinkled with a thousand instructions, a thousand duties, a thousand rules. He was laden heavy with duty, an indispensable preparation for the future of a true gentleman of his position. But he was still little and had small needs of sweetness.

The grand palazzo where he lived swarmed with servants. It was always very busy with all the dinners, lunches, and receptions which animated the brightly illuminated salons where the important families came together. They came with their swishing garments and impeccable tailcoats. The frescoed ceilings reflected their colors on the snowy shoulders of the women, some of whom were beautiful and some of whom less so.

At the beginning of the evening events, even though he was very small, he made an appearance for a brief few moments. He was dressed in a little custom made velvet suit. He was exhibited as a symbol of perfect love, the yearned-for heir to a great surname, the proof of a certain continuity.

But he didn't know it. His eyes lowered, dazed from all the compliments, the kisses and pats on the cheek, he would finally climb the stairs clinging to the governess's neck. He only knew that the great salon would be his once again in the morning after the party.

In the daylight hours as he played, he would watch Antonio, the faithful old butler, at work. Antonio would drag a long stick which had at either end affixed a heavy iron with cushioned padding, attempting with exhausting motions forward and backward to remove from the flooring the indication of the lively party the night before. Gregorio was a child, and couldn't help himself but jump up and down on the moving iron slab as Antonio laughed joyfully.

He was born, unfortunately, into a context of traditions and duties. It was a golden world kept alive with rites by now worn away, economic possibilities exploited to the max, and compromises masquerading as needs. A gilded environment closed into itself, its logic in stark contrast with a social context that was shifting.

Their life of that time, earned day after day in a world already in the past, was made up of the use of inherited and tenaciously maintained privileges. The use of lands and homes spread far and wide, reinforced with the logics of borders and of opportunity, defended like an unconquerable fortress.

But the world around them was changing. The child was growing up and bursting out with a robust will from his golden circle.

He began to understand and spurn all that was coming to him from a past that was not his. He resisted the idea that for him, an uninformed descendant of a heroic commander of adventure, everything should be easy or taken for granted.

He wanted to feel he was a boy like all the others. He sought a normal boyhood and for this he became affectionately known as a bit of a rebel. His parents used his young age to excuse his behavior, hoping that very soon and very certainly he would come back to his senses. They would say, "for blood is not water". (This is like the English saying "blood is thicker than water" in the sense of "the apple does not fall far from the tree.")

Gregorio's first horseback riding lessons summoned the whole family to the garden, perfectly positioned above the Sotto Fosso, an unpaved road lined with wickedly sharp gravel. Since Gregorio was too small for a horse, he was given a stubborn donkey indifferent to the privilege it had been given in being promoted.

The calm and good natured donkey allowed the boy to climb up in the saddle, and even permitted itself to be led a few steps forward, giving off the illusion of being resigned to its task. But suddenly, with a lightning quick jerk, the donkey flung him onto the gravel that welcomed him with cuts and scratches, reducing everything in a cloud of dust.

'He who perseveres, wins!', they exclaimed from the garden. Between scrapes and bruises everywhere, he followed with another attempt to demonstrate his perseverance. Again and again, until becoming a perfect horseman.

In the years to come he rode marvelous racehorses, a passion received from his uncle who participated in some of the largest horse races with prestigious horses and professional jockeys.

Gregorio went on long horseback rides with the stable hand, Giulio. While they were out they had games of ruzzola, a throwing game similar to frisbee, on the hairpin turns of the road at

Villalba. They made excursions in the woods, and in October they attended the festivals of the effervescent young 'mosto' wine. In his outings at Sotto Fosso arose his initial political sympathies. Gregorio had an admiration without boundary for his father, who was soaring towards an important political career.

His father was initially the Mayor of Orvieto, the city of his birth. The world was changing but the little city of Orvieto sitting like a castle above the cliff walls resisted. Those who dared to leap towards unbounded horizons became considered reckless, a bit traitor and a bit rebel, but in reality they were admired and envied.

His father was then elected to Parliament in Rome, actively involved in valuing everyone's rights regardless of social class.

Every summer the extended family gathered together. Gregorio's elderly grandfather officiated the great house that swarmed with grownups and little ones. There were regular lunches with the Bishop and the local authorities. Children were absolutely forbidden from these events, and were given lunch earlier, in advance of the adults.

The servants tried to control the children's exuberant liveliness, which was made greater by a curiosity in the prohibited lunches. There were many cousins who played together. Gregorio was calm and reflective. But of all the children, his vivacious cousin Carlo Alberto was the most enthralling, and also the most dangerously unpredictable. Usually during an important lunch he climbed up very high on the outside palazzo wall, as far as a little window that belonged to the dining room.

Inside, everything was perfect. The servants glided about in silence. The waitresses were lovely in their headbands and pretty aprons. The butler in his white gloves presided over the scene, composed and aware of his rank. And there up high, the malevolent Carlo Alberto sought, by hurling a little stone, to strike the Bishop with bullseye precision.

Often the family organized outings in the countryside. The ladies and children went off in various buggies. The daredevils went on horseback. Every time it was a different destination, Pianociano, Selvella, Campo Ricco. They had snacks on the banks of the river Rivalcale.

The ladies were seated on the ground with their dresses forming colorful circles around them. The chivalrous young men brought forth every sort of gallantry. And the children, finally unleashed from the shiny parquet floors and forbidden salons, were able to let off some steam.

This was their life, theirs by natural right, limited to those who had the fortune to be born in that gilded sphere of a world that existed for the few. And he was part of it. Long horseback rides up to Campo Ricco, the rests, the horse quivering, the fragrances of the forest, the wind that caressed his face. This land was his, the taste of figs just off the tree, the calm greeting of the farmers, everything seemed eternal, it was his right.

His mother's cool sweetness contrasted with the tenderness of his father. Gregorio's heart would swell with proud love as he looked at his father, handsome in his splendid uniform, with his hand tightly in his own.

When his father would go to Rome, often he combined business with pleasure and took Gregorio with him to Parliament. Despite the long waits in the famous Transatlantico corridor of Montecitorio, he had the opportunity to meet important people in innumerable handshakes. His fear of getting lost in that enormous unknown place was assuaged by the reassurance of the strong hand of his father squeezing his. Hearing "This is my son" rendered him ecstatic, and certainly no one had ever had a father so sweet and also so important.

Since he was a bit delicate in health, his parents decided to move to the sea, to Gaeta, a marvelous period for the family. His father continued his work in Parliament and in politics.

Gregorio, first a son of the Italian Lupa organization, and then a young fascist, participated in the youth exercises at the forum of Mussolini and won a medal in track and field.

He believed in the values of fascism, they had become his values. He believed in Italy, and dreamed of enrolling in the Navy while he frolicked around the gulf of Gaeta in the little boat. Everyone knew him. His mother watched his daring antics with trepidation from the balcony, dreaming to see him in a long career as a Captain, handsome in his white uniform.

He wasn't a fan of studying, he just went to school because it was one of his duties. He loved the countryside, the green of the forests, the wild runs along the hillsides covered in soft and aromatic grasses. And he always looked forward to summer in the big house.

His life had been one event after another, some tragic. There was the death of his maternal grandmother in a road accident. At the time the occurrence was rather uncommon and rare, since cars were truly few and far between. The accident happened just at the entrance to the town. Now in the curve where the car overturned there is a cross to mark the memory. The cross is there but few by now know why, as so much time has passed.

During the winter season he would stay in Rome, since his father was busier than ever with politics. He yearned for summer, aways with the same joyful anxiousness, when all the family would reunite in the big house like a castle on the hill. Perched on the north side of the little town, the balcony and the windows opened wide onto a scenario that was breathtaking to say the least. So many little hilltowns poked up in the distance: Fabro, Ficulle, Montegabbione, Monteleone, and on the clearest days on the horizon even the towers of Citta della Pieve.

Forests and farmhouses rested on little hills like fortresses defending a peaceful life. The tall ravines of clay seemed almost wounds inflicted to dampen so much beauty. The gray of the clay slid down between the green of the forest, it seemed naked and only stray puffs of yellow scotch broom softened and refined the gray.

Down below was the river Paglia, an irregular riverbed that cut the whole valley with its meandering. The river followed straight lines and capricious curves, its bright white stones quietly tumbled down the banks. They were silent witnesses to the river's furious impetuosity that could arrive unexpectedly and unstoppably.

A staircase led down from the house into the garden. In one corner was a little grotto where a small Madonna still smiled, more for habit than for willingness, her sky blue cloak a bit faded.
A weeping willow graced the grass next to her.

Rose bushes gave off their intense and permeating fragrance, fiercely protecting with their thorns the other flowers. Even so, hydrangeas pushed up against them, trying to earn the prize of being the biggest and most beautiful.

In the middle of the garden was a large flower bed overflowing with tulips of intense and varied color near an imposing spruce tree. Benches and armchairs waited to receive the rustle of long skirts. Tea was served between laughs, anecdotes, and the latest news.

The rest of the town lived in their shadow, trying to peer through a barrier as thick as a forest of waving bamboo, for a small taste of this faraway and prohibited world.

This was his world: a multitude of cousins, a little kingdom in miniature, a future without difficulty, planned, secure, and rosy.

Life flowed along calmly.

1930'S ORVIETO DURING GREGORIO'S CHILDHOOD

Italy meanwhile was living a period full of splendor. In Orvieto, the city castled on the cliffs, the Women's Gymnastic Academy was inaugurated. This was a national avantgarde complex where young girls would dedicate themselves to difficult athletic disciplines.

The social life of the town often focused around the Academy, as it was a leap of unstoppable quality for the city. Beautiful girls livened up the noble Via del Duomo, whose sublime beauty enhanced the scene. The Academy contributed an impulse of social innovation. On one side was a world privileged by birth, and on another a world that began to see differences as less severe. It seemed possible there to study ways to close the gaps.

Artisanal craftsmanship flourished now. A land that had been purely agricultural transformed in a more variegated context. There was no longer simply the privileged class of landowners separate from an invisible peasant class.

Other hopes and perspectives became clear on the horizon. Little by little the cliff town of Orvieto became less insular, and began to glimpse the possibility to make a leap towards a tomorrow that was beginning to take flight.

Gregorio remembered like a nightmare his highschool diploma, the sleepless nights, and his graduation. It was a little step towards his life path, an obligatory stop in order to have a future. But the first winds of war were starting, a war invoked and desired by the Italian people, who were united in the choice of a better life.

His father's political life and career had forged him into a boy of strong and resolute character. He had absolute and total conviction in fascist principles, and an immense love for his country, his family, and God.

GREGORIO'S MILITARY SERVICE

On September 8, 1943, he had 19 years under his belt and no uncertainty whatsoever. Only the awareness that he must do something, anything, for Italy. It wasn't a difficult or challenging decision. And so without expectations, without illusions, and without hopes, he entered the official military zone of Orvieto and enrolled in the Repubblica Sociale Italiana, the RSI.

He was in a military unit for just a few days, in the barracks together with so many young men like him. Some were friends from school and childhood. All were armed with the same faith and huge love for an Italy which they saw as betrayed, vilified, violated.[14] His uniform was too big for him, and just as big was his impatience to set off and fight for his country.

Their love for an Italy in peril made the boys aware that every minute might be too long. They wanted to fight for and defend their country, to redeem even with their lives the disgrace of a surrender that had no dignity, a clearance sale on an Italy that had been feared and envied, the sale of a people capable of huge endeavors and enormous sacrifices.

His first military actions were in the Garfagnana region of Tuscany. They were young students in an unequal war with the awareness of betrayal in every corner. They knew how fleeting could be the memory of someone who until yesterday loved and believed in Italy, the memory of those who had chosen a life of desertion to a life of duty and loyalty to the oath of defending and honoring their own Nation.

He went to an exhausting training at the school for student officers in Fontanellato, in Emilia Romagna. Impatience ate at their hearts, for they were ready to endure long draining marches, deprivations and exertion in an ever more true and important conviction. They were the 'young future soldiers', a complete and honest cohesion that later on in their lives, despite persecution and separation from one another, would remain intact forever in each of them.

They marched through the streets of Fontanellato, brimming with pride, singing the song "Giovinezza" among hostile or wary gazes. They were tired but their voices showed their loyalty, love and hope. With them the silent streets were filled with a merry challenge, here were the last true men.

He was a second lieutenant and his next destination was Mortirolo, an inhospitable and impenetrable mountain in the central Alps. The command station was at Monno, the maneuvers were continuing, always more difficult in an unknown and rugged land, the stronghold of the local people who knew every ravine and every path.

It was an unequal struggle. On the one hand youths like Gregorio armed with faith and determination, and on the other hand youths confident of their sure predominance - they weren't fighting battles, they seemed more firing at pigeons.

Little bands of soldiers like Gregorio's went up towards the peak of the mountain between exhausting marches in unknown places. Often they were blessed by the fog which, hiding them, gifted them another day of life. But sometimes the wind unpredictably left them without cover, in scarce vegetation and on a barren and treacherous slope

Bands of soldiers like Gregorios went toward the top where lay the confident young deserters.

The deserters were protected by trenches from the first world war, moving from one post to another, across walkways dug out by those early first world war heroes. They dominated the entire slope and from there the deserters would begin the slaughter.

The deserters spread death with little risk to themselves, killing soldiers like Gregorio without the courage of a true battle where you look your enemy in the eye. They created extensive blood-baths with systematic precision. They weren't defending any-thing - surely it was not Italy they defended, nor did they defend honor. The deserters killed just for the pleasure of it. They killed for the pleasure of wiping out those like Gregorio whose loyalty and love for Italy made the deserters feel inconsequential by comparison.

Gregorio saw days of glory and of sacrifice. He didn't know how long he would be there. He was strong in his loyalty, proud and aware of the stronger forces of deserters that faced him, the de-serters who had been bribed by their future allies. He contrasted them with his dignity, his honor, his unmuted and unchanged courage, offering his life as his last and ultimate gift.

He was honored to wear the red M of the Tagliamento regiment, gifted to him by those who still believed in loyalty. The heroic and legendary Tagliamento, the military campaign in Russia, a real war with real enemies, heroic deeds fought for the greatness of Italy.

Gregorio, you were a soldier of the Tagliamento division and you remained so all the way until your death.

SURRENDER BY THE RSI AND ESCAPE

And then came the surrender, a surrender customized by Commander Zuccari. All of you were like sons to him, he protected you, defended and honored you, all of you. In a long line of youths with your Commander at the lead, you marched. You were not defeated men. Your adversaries followed you from a distance, and in a resurgence of forgotten loyalty they did not intervene, they did not shoot. They watched you march and they measured your greatness, like the last bastion of an Italy that destroyed itself, the ultimate extreme defense against betrayal.

The sounds of your songs vibrated in the air. Eyes full of tears, you sang the lyrics of some of the old Fascist songs, "Le donne non ci vogliono più bene perché portiamo la camicia nera, giovinezza, primavera di bellezza….Women don't love us anymore because we wear the black shirts, youth, the spring of beauty."

It was spring. What a difference from your arrival when you still had the desire to fight, to use the last breath of life for your beautiful Italy.

Only bitterness remained now, you didn't understand or know anything or anyone. There in that valley you gave your last salute, burned your weapons, said the last farewell to friends with the awareness that you would never see them again. Each of you pursued his own path, aware of being outcasts, and that the enemy could be anywhere.

You found it extraordinary that in some people goodness still dwelled, like that family that took you in during the night. They dressed you in old clothes since you had burned your uniform to wipe out any possible reprisal from helping the enemy. How your situation had changed, you were now prey to be hunted.

People who yesterday had given wing to your song were now invisible. You were now the absolute enemy. Your feet sought to rest in hiding places far from towns, like a wild animal who avoids civilization.

During the night your mind was flooded with images from the past...your parents, the big house full of life, the last visit of your mother there at Monno. Her desperate hugs revealed to you how fragile and defenseless she was without the protection of her golden world.

Your papà, the blue of his eyes, the sweetness of his hand on your hair, where was he? Would your parents have escaped from all this destruction? You wandered without any goal and without any hope.

Finally you arrived in Padova in search of your uncle. You were afraid to show up at your uncle's house because you feared you might compromise his own safety. But it was your only chance at survival.

You arrived in the dark of the night and found a hiding place under the stairs. The doorman discovered you during his usual checks, not recognizing you at first. You had a wild beard and were dressed in clothes that are too big. But then the doorman recognized you, embraced you, and he hid you in the coal cellar while you waited for your uncle to return.

And when your uncle arrived, he tells you all that you would never have wanted to hear.

Your father and mother are locked up in the prison of San Vittore in Milan awaiting a verdict. Your aunt Agnese, sweet and fragile, and your uncle Arrigo are without a home, wandering continually between one convent and another, depending on other people's mercy.

You feel powerless, destroyed, guilty for even being alive. You think about your mother, how she was before, and you cannot imagine what she might be like now. She was not even allowed to share a cell with your father, she was alone. Her delicate hands searched in the garbage for something to eat. She received compassion from the other prisoners, and mercy from the nuns who tried to lessen her suffering.

She was allowed only brief conversations, conversations which were heavily spied on. They wanted to know where you were. With ridicule and sarcasm, they lavished cruelties upon your parents freely, they called them dirty fascists. Their only crime was to have a son as a soldier in the Tagliamento.

You stayed in Padova only a few days, just enough time to organize your trip back home. On the road you realize just how much Italy has changed. There were the victors, so many of them lately. Then there were the nostalgics, those busy using any means possible to assume for themselves a new life, denying that which they had been.

Then there were those, the worst of all, who used any type of trickery to demonstrate that their redemption was complete, tricking the rest of the world by recounting imaginary persecutions and tortures, impositions and extortions. Many became the new political class, full of imagination, creativity, and heroic gestures - elements indispensable for governing the new, free Italy.

You never arrived home to Allerona. You didn't have a home anymore, and you would have had no one to greet you. Or better said, many awaited you but with intentions decidedly different from what you might have liked.

Most of the peasant class had been woken. They were "liberated" now, and to see themselves as such they even broke down the big front door of the great house, they burned, stole, and organized a demonic destruction. They crushed your historic photographs under their heels, they divided up your furniture, a long parade carried it away in triumph, one took a bed, another a couch. The golden console tables became a picturesque resting place for jugs of wine. Anyone who protests is punished: the women shaved bald and covered in tar, the men, who are few by now, are beaten with wine jugs and insults.

Everything was avenged. The charitable acts Aunt Agnese had done for the weakest became seen as arrogant superiority towards the peasants. They forgot the good that was received in a long line of acts articulated with hatred. The documents in the great house, witness to its history, fed a great bonfire in the garden. They burned without mercy. Wiping everything out became imperative, it was necessary to eliminate everything.

They deluded themselves into thinking they had become the leaders. But they didn't know and they didn't understand that their actions were trademarks that characterized them: infamy, ignorance and self-deception.

What made you what you are - elegance, manners, principles of honest rectitude, and loyalty - these things are not available for conquest. Instead, the bandits' deeds so clearly outlined by a hatred of a race came only from a sense of inadequacy. And you would know nothing of inadequacy.

The great house becomes transformed into barracks for the carabinieri. The impressive salon, the delicate colors on the wall paper and the colonnade with rose branches, refuse to grace that which no longer exists.

The great salon had been divided into cells for detainees of low association. Blasphemies, profanities, and curses resounded there in an unpleasant clamor. Thus the new world and new society arrived. Farewell to the gilded world. Here instead was the absence of conviction that nothing could be harmed. Forces much more powerful plotted in the shadows - hatred of class, unchained ambition at any cost, betrayals, about-turns of character, and compromises. Everything was permitted.

Little by little a deep patina darkened the colors, hiding their delicate beauty. Strips of ripped wallpaper fluttered, hanging off the wall. That wallpaper hid its past, witness to a world made of harmony and grace. There are no longer sweet reunions or tea sipped slowly or swishing silks and light hands that brush the piano keys, the music echoing off the marble of the furniture, spreading a harmony of notes and elegance.

You didn't have anything anymore. No house, no green fields where the spring grain flowed in waves like the sea, the thick forests where you knew every angle, every path. You had become a being that, in order to live, must forget. You have no point of reference. Up there on Mortirolo Pass remained your honor, your friends, your hopes, your conviction. Your faith had been shaken but not your ideals.

You would have done all which you did for Italy over again. But now you had some reservations about the Italian people. You had believed them to be cohesive, faithful, and committed. You had been a dreamer.

Finally the new world could take that which it thought it was owed, even so far as to wipe out traditions and rights of descendancy and inheritance. It was a new and powerful day, one which didn't want to recognize traditions, or the past. These were all the ingredients that were necessary to know, love and above all understand one's neighbor as a human being, to respect him in his limits and not to hate him because he was born in a context different from one's own.

Your constant and imperative preoccupation was to flee from this Italy that disavowed you and that you no longer understood.

A little airplane carried you far from your Umbria.

Even the little airplane that carried you to Sardinia confronted together with you the mystery of a voyage perhaps without hope, without a tomorrow. Few people were with you on that plane but all of them shared your ideals. They too had offered up to Italy the only resource they had: their life. They too were completely absorbed by their recent past, and had little hopes for a future. In their dignity and their honor they were labeled as traitors and losers. But they were the true moral champions.

When a war ends, the winners write the history. New generations take over, and they coin other terms that are convenient and full of imagination. What we viewed as betrayal was for them simply the choice to take the easy path. The Anglo Americans were formally the absolute enemy to all Italians. But the Anglo Americans became embraced in the flash of an eye by many Italians as allies and liberators. It was simply convenient and safe. It was also cowardly. At the end of the war, the new Italian leaders, those who had switched sides, created for themselves fancy sounding names, unblemished histories, new birth, a liberated and pure Italy.

He who had fired like a coward from behind became a heroic defender, champion of the longed for liberation. He now had a path open to high positions in the Italian government. A new Italy, satisfied and proud, aimed towards lofty summits. Finally the people were sovereign, creators who could choose whether to be a part of the satellites of Mother Russia or a colony of the Anglo American people.

Your airplane landed in jerks and screeches at the edge of its limits, at the airport of Elmas in Sardinia. Your little group parts ways, trying to overcome emotion. They have nothing, so they offer each other the last possible illusion of,"we will see each other again...courage!"

For you the only mooring place for the time being was the Sardinian town of Capoterra, where your father's brother resides. There you remained for some time, trying to drown your anguish with continuous hard work.

The back breaking work helps you to not think. You are afraid to think about the bloody slopes of Mortirolo and the last words to your comrade dying in your arms, "I beg you to hang on, they are coming to help us." You tried to stop the bleeding with your hands. His whisper was always more faint, but you pressed on his wounds. You knew that it was useless but you refused to accept it. Twenty years old is far too young to die.

There was a last agonizing salute of your comrades before they surrendered, convinced by a priest in a fraternal cassock. They trusted his captivating smile, the simpleness of his frock, and his promise to save their lives. "Kids, the war is over, if you surrender I will guarantee your safety." But in the new Italy, giving one's word and loyalty didn't exist any more. And you couldn't even trust priests, the ones one would expect to represent ethical values.

But your comrades didn't know this, they didn't know that giving one's word was an antiquated concept. And so, in agreement, they descended from the Hotel Franceschetti all the way to Rovetta, deluded but not knowing it. They were imprisoned first in the elementary schools where the torture began. Stripped of what little they had, they were undressed, humiliated, and derided. Some began to no longer believe they would be saved. Others persisted in believing in the priest's promise.

But it wasn't so. Only one of them was saved, the youngest. The other forty-three of them, the oldest barely more than 20 years old, were taken and led naked just behind the cemetery at Roventta. And there in groups of five they were barbarically riddled with merciless and precise bullets.

The "heroic" partisans who slaughtered them, so fearless and satisfied, collected the poor martyred bodies and threw them in a pile of animal fertilizer. The traitorous priest, ordained in the name of God, tried every night and day to wipe away the innocent blood that stained his hands. Every night and day until his death.

Up there towards the sky, on the ridge of the mountain, marched the heroic boys of Rovetta. On their chest shone the Red M badge, the leather tassels of their berets moving at every gust of wind, their last cry of "Long live Italy!" resounding towards the blue heavens.

They are still there, martyrs in the wind. The servant of God will hear their voices singing the song "Giovinezza", or "Youth", and will see in the poppies the red of their spilled blood, for an Italy that was destroyed. The grass will once again cover the ridge, and tired footsteps will crush it, bringing forth a flower, to witness that their sacrifice was not in vain. Many people still remember, honor and respect these young betrayed soldiers.

Even today the descendants of those confident partisan "heroes" of deceptions sneak around like their forefathers. At night and on all fours so as not to be seen, they destroy, stain and desecrate an empty tomb of the Tagliamento. But the true heroes are still there. It is not enough to desecrate and destroy. Nothing will propel these desecrators towards heaven. Their place instead is there crawling in the shadows, their small mindedness holds them firmly anchored to the lowest rung of humanity.

Only chosen souls can aspire to boundless heavens, to immense glories. During the night you drowned your anguish in a bottomless well. During the day you wore yourself out in your hopelessness with exhausting physical labor, so you wouldn't have the strength or time to think about memories.

You felt desperate in this new land. But at least here in Sardinia there were no wild beasts to flush out, no safari hunts for sinister fascists organized by the State. The Sardinian people are wonderful, intense in their loyalty and in their sense of honor, in their respect for humans. They are a people who carefully make the appropriate judgment. They are not influenced by hearsay, but by what they see for themselves.

You are that which you demonstrated yourself to me, not judged and condemned at a glance but a man to be understood and evaluated in the present time. You are who you are: proud to respect your past and traditions, with pride and determination.

You eventually found a bit of peace in a newly discovered land. You took control of your life, of your youth, you were finally reunited with your parents. Your mother sought solace behind the shield of protection that is her deep faith. Your father was surprisingly cheerful and accommodating, his ideals indelible and intact.

The three of you tried to avoid talking and remembering. The past was still too painful, too recent. The aching wound was still there and no words could lessen the deep pain. Your native world was far away. Your uncle and aunt had returned to the great house in Umbria, but nothing was as before.

Softened a bit in Umbria by now was the drunkenness of hatred and revenge. The conformists, dragged from the moment of collective fury, gave way to some regret. They restored back to your family some of the furniture and objects - not everything, but some - that they had pillaged in the name of hate and of that longed for "liberation". Some furnishings resume their original place. Many townspeople begin to think that, all things considered, they were better off before the war.

The victors soon lost a bit of their demented splendor. Yes, they had stolen furniture and lands, and in doing so they thought they had destroyed the golden world they hated. Yes, they become the ruling class of the country, proud of their lightning quick ascent. But in the base of their soul they were aware of not being able to embrace elegance or appreciation for beautiful things. They knew they were incapable of that touch of sensitivity developed over the centuries, and of all that is innate and which distinguishes a true gentleman.

In Sardinia you found a few friends. More often you found people like you, fugitives in search of peace. Here in Sardinia, they too found hope for a future and respect.

Often you came to take a swim at the tidal pool. You felt old, inadequate. You wanted desperately to insert yourself in the joy of those young friends. It was tough, even though the difference between your age and theirs was minimal. For them the past is a refuge, but for you it is an abyss of pain. The future was reduced to the immediate, and tomorrow was an unknown.

GREGORIO'S PERSPECTIVE

One morning like so many others, you headed to the tidal pool. The sky was clear, the silver flight of the mullets danced on the water. You struggled to place your feet on the razor sharp seashells. Each careful step was like a thought held with difficulty so as not to touch on painful memories. Behind you you heard a tentative and unsure step, a "ciao" more whispered than spoken. Quickly, you turned and saw a small harmonious figure with a hint of a timid smile. A cascade of blonde hair concealed and hid my face at every rush of wind.

You rose and firmly shook, while the voice of Attico said, "Piera, this is my new friend Gregorio."

You didn't look at me and I didn't want to look at you either. I actually ignored you completely and continued to stare at a point out in the distance. You felt old and I felt small and childish, but aware of my beauty. I felt that I represent all that you would like to dream of, but also all that you cannot aspire to. You had nothing to offer me, you felt simply a shell from which life has stripped your heart and dreams.

But we had tranquil days together. Days passed with quarrels, frowns and laughs, suppressed instincts. You were kind but deliberately emotionless, our interactions interwoven with prolonged silences. You turned your gaze toward the acrobatics of the mullet fish. You struggled to not rest your gaze on me, occasionally succeeding but with difficulty. You strained to respond to my questions with light sarcasm, while concentrating on smothering the desire to caress my hair.

When I would arrive at the beach in the morning, you held back your longing to run and meet me. In waiting to be able to see me again, you manufactured any means so as not to realize or see who you are, a man thirsty for love, a man needful of dreams and hopes.

You turned desperately, instead, to any kind of rationalizing logic. You decided that I deserved a different life from what you might be able to offer me. You thought I should have certain hopes, a certain future, a life which you, in your condition, cannot guarantee me. And so you wallowed in a jealousy masked as total indifference. You feel dislike for Enzo, handsome and sculpted, kind and affectionate. And for Piero, thoughtful and loyal. You think that he overshadows you with his calm steadfastness, his dedication.

We had outings together in the boat, joking around. And then unexpectedly, your total capitulation, the unconditional surrender to a feeling that, despite your determined wish and your arguments full of solid logic, proclaimed victory.

You declared to me in this way your feelings and the reasons you wanted to hide them. You confessed that you camouflaged them under an exasperated indifference. What a useless effort! How many days had we lost! But I smiled at you and said, then, and for always, 'I am also in love with you.'

How many times, in our long life together, did we remember that moment and those happy days?

Continually, as if it were today.

We took long walks together in Cagliari, where our preferred place was the botanical garden. You would show me the vast variety of plants. When you spoke to me of the wondrous properties of the soil, emotion weakened your voice. You told me about your lands that were no longer yours, of your world, of your green region Umbria, and slowly, on tiptoe, I entered into your life.

I knew that your past had marked your character forever. I was aware that to live with you would have been a back and forth between infinite heights and painful falls. But it didn't matter where or how, I wanted only to share my life with you, to sense the protection and love you gave me. I was certain that I would never again experience a love so great.

You took me to meet your parents. Your father was friendly and smiling. Your mother, Ada, however, was too courteous. Too friendly, too everything. She was enveloped in a sense of cold-ness and the forbidden. She was an invisible enemy that I wasn't capable of recognizing. We were from different worlds; hers was a propriety forged over the centuries.

I was 18 years old, and I believed that the world was mine. I believed I had free license. But it was not to be, none of this was to be. In that world I was rejected. I wasn't good enough. I didn't have illustrious ancestors or an important surname. I was equipped only with infinite true love. Far too little.

And so our love was obstructed. Your family and your world were deaf to our feelings. Traditions and ambitions were what counted. Marriages were arranged and reasoned based on land borders and adjacent properties. I became, despite myself, the protagonist in a feud against true love.

Ours was a powerless rebellion. You tried to reassure me, with a hope that even in you was wavering, "You will see, everything will work out, I will be able to convince them that you are the most important thing to me, I will never give up on you, they will need to understand…"

How many words, how many hopes crushed as soon as they were born, how many days did we spend seeking a path forward. And then suddenly, but clearly very well planned, your reentry to your region of origin, Umbria, was arranged.

Even a great love cannot compete against intricate schemes put in place by master strategists. These strategists had, in their own lives, put aside their own sentiments for practical benefits. What counted were important family names, nobility, and obligation. Sometimes ruined fortunes were reassembled from marriages crafted simply to enrich holdings and preserve traditions.

LIFE IN SARDINIA AFTER GREGORIO'S DEPARTURE

Your departure was marked by a goodbye as agonizing as if it were a farewell forever. Your hand dried my tears, your voice whispered, "I beg you, my love, I will speak with my aunts and uncles, I will convince them. Wait for me, we will make our dreams come true, we will get married, we will live forever together, wait for me."

How many battles did they wage in a war of self-interest, against a boy and a girl armed only with infinite love. They were armed with aristocratic titles and ancient logical reasonings. And we only had love.

In those times, proprietary conveniences trumped all else. They reinforced in you the certainty that you couldn't offer me anything, a tactic appropriate to the most cunning minds. They loaded you with responsibilities that were bigger than you, folding in your sense of guilt for the destruction of the golden world that no longer existed. They fueled your desperate belief that you would only be clipping my wings by offering me a love without a future.

Maybe it was the distance or the letters that were always more sporadic. Letters sent that never arrived. My desperation was always deeper. I had my first doubts, and finally the certainty that I was in a one way love. Darkly resigned, I could only face that my hopes were impossible, and that it was not to be. I had glimpsed Paradise, that which remained with me was only the dream to think how it would have been to be able to enter and live there.

My life continued and I began to work as a model. I wore magnificent dresses and soft furs with a silky heat in short runway shows. I moved between the towns of Nuoro, Macomer, and so many other wonderful places, places rarely possessing any inner tranquility.

One of the places I went was the town of Orgosolo, the cradle of Sardinian banditry and haven of hardened and merciless delinquents. Just the name would arouse fear.

The road that led from Macomer found its way to Nuoro, and was patrolled by carabinieri on horseback. The countryside was peppered with cork trees. Their trunks were stripped of the precious cork which had covered their nudity, revealing a velvety brown color. And there up high was the town of Orgosolo, a tenacious fortress, a threatening presence and culture which was very little understood.

In the main piazza of Orgosolo a little group of men gathered. They were curious about this rather rare occasion, the arrival of our car. Even more so they were curious about us ladies with our fitted tops, white bootleg pants that complimented the figure, and caps on our heads tilted to cover one side of the face.

We got out of the car cautiously. We expected a cheery welcome along the lines of rifle shots, and we headed tentatively towards the only coffee bar in town. My high heels battled with the street pavement, and it was impossible to avoid swaying my hips as I walked.

Two stern men came out of the bar, their faces hidden by thick black beards. They held their hands resting on their hearts, and gave a hint of a bow at our presence. I felt like a true queen, and in those men I saw the highest form of chivalry. Their reputation was of being bandits and delinquents, but they were true men who defended their trampled rights, who respected and honored women.

Many continental Italians, "respectable" people, don't have within them as much dignity as there was in even one hair of the beard of those marvelous citizens of Orgosolo, the legacy of a chosen people.

Those were wondrous times in a Sardinia that no longer exists.

The Emerald Coast is today a modern shadow of what it once was. A natural paradise created by God's hands, today it is desecrated in the name of money. It offers places that are stylish, where every means and strategy tries to prolong the fleeing moments, a reality that satisfies no one.

The places where I lived, instead, had white sand striking against the blue sea and little coves. Through the clear water one could see the mysterious depths, stones bathed by the waves shimmered with variegated colors.

There were kilometers of beaches inhabited only by lentiscus trees and mediterranean forests. The tree trunks stretched out toward the land, twisted themselves in a thousand forms, some graceful, some demoniacal, offering to the wind their total obedience, for there the wind is king.

Rosemary bushes spread an intense perfume, intoxicating us in waves of flowers as delicate as breaths. At any rise of the wind a fine perfumed dust every so lightly colored violet was released into the air.

In my Sardinia, every angle and every perspective seemed a hymn to beauty. Every inhabitant was the deserving caretaker of such an elevated harmony.

The years passed, but my love and my regret remained there, intact, sheltered deep in my heart. Every hope had been self-destroyed. Time went by emptily and relentlessly.

Then suddenly one day I noticed your motorcycle parked in front of where I was working. Inescapably and immediately began a torturous swinging between hope, delusion, and tears.

We had brief and strictly random encounters. The beating of my heart suffocated in an aloof handshake. Carefully chosen words won in a dance of apathy, randomness, and hypocrisy.

"How are you? I see you are doing well, I am here for a few days, I'm happy to have seen you," you said. And then an avalanche of insignificant things articulated out of pride to try to at least have the upper hand, to be the most detached and apathetic possible. A handshake.

And then my effort to not turn around to see you even for one moment more.

The tears crushed forward, deaf to any reasoning. My heart beat wildly full, instead, of other unsaid words, "I didn't forget you even though I gave up, but if you look in my eyes, if you tell me to wait, if only I didn't see you so cold and distant, I would give you all of my life in exchange for your love, not a dream of eternity but even just one day with you, which would fill the void of an entire life."

But these words were all unsaid. I would have wanted to shout my love to you, but pride rendered me paralyzed. I was convinced that if you truly loved me, you would have fought until your last breath to be able to live with me.

My letters had been without any response. Our meetings were now always more rare and formal. Rational logic began its slow work on the destruction of dreams and hopes, the thought that perhaps my love had been true, but yours not. The mirage of a great love that for such a long time had been hidden away and eaten away was in full demolition mode.

I began to look around me, and I moved my interest to other shores. I began to yearn for a child. Something that was all mine, on which I could heap completely all my love.

I identified the victim, a gorgeous boy about my age. For the first time in my life I gave more importance to physical appearance than to all the traits I had identified as ideal in a man. And I viewed him more as a friend than as a life partner.

In reality, I ignored the thousand signs and just as many alarm bells. He was too confident in his physical charm. But he was a beautiful wrapping on an empty package.

Deaf to any plea, blind to any evidence, confident in my detachedness, and heavily vaccinated against every human weakness, I decided to get married. A marriage that was well thought out, without any other prospects, free of economic calculations. Just another marriage without a future. I wanted my own house, but above all I wanted a child.

And so the date was set. The big day dreamed of by every woman in love became the tombstone of a dream buried deep in my heart.

WEDDING PREPARATIONS

I asked for a simple ceremony. My mother understood but imposed upon me the white dress. She wanted to redeem what was missing from my First Communion. I agreed, but my state of mind remained the same as before.

My only excuse was to think of changing my destiny by modifying my principles, betraying every belief. I had days full of anxious hesitation, and nights full of bad dreams and fears.

The night before the wedding I dreamed of Gregorio. He came up to me, his gaze was desperate. His hand outstretched to indicate my white gown. I looked down at a marvelous white dress stained by black ink. I sought help from the man who was beside me, my fiance. He was motionless, an unknown face with a detached and indifferent composure. I desperately tried to blot the ink with my veil. But the stains became ever bigger and darker.

I woke up from this dream at the mercy of a deep anxiety mixed with a sensation of powerlessness. I was afraid, I had a bad feeling that was anything but reassuring, Damp with a cold sweat, I took solace in my mother's arms. Her perfume, her warm embrace, the certainty that she would always be there rendered me a bit calmer.

"I beg you, don't get married, he's not the man for you. It doesn't matter that all the guests are already here, together we will face the consequences. I beg you, don't go ahead with this wedding," she said.

But I went ahead.

I was married in the church of Santa Anna in Cagliari. I ascended the stairs on the arm of my father. We passed in front of the Madonna whom I had many times asked for the miracle of living forever with Gregorio. With the excuse of adjusting my dress we made a little stop in front of her. I confronted her glassy gaze. I left at her feet my baggage of resentment and regret. I left there the accusation that even the Lord who can do anything had capitulated in the name of earthly reasons, conveniences, and class affiliations.

Stupidly relieved of all of this, I went towards the altar. The clicking of my heels echoed the beating of my heart. I saw the trembling of the candles and smelled the intense fragrance of the flowers. I was an observer and not a protagonist. I was shaping my destiny without conviction. I was summoning up a minimum of loyalty to promise that I would be a good wife.

I was one of the world's many wives headed to the altar with the conviction that love would come later. I knew he wasn't the man I wanted but with time you would change him. I was reasoning full of logic. Clearly I had absorbed much more than I had thought of a world that had pushed me away without appeal.

MARRIED LIFE

I did not need to work much to be a good wife. My tasks were rather simple: work, take on all the responsibilities, and respect the duties of the head of family. I was immediately pregnant with the longed for child.

Everything became more tolerable: the superficiality of my husband and his total lack of absolutely any responsibility. He had a sick charm, and a character that lent itself to any compromise. He was pleasant and intelligent. His physical appearance was captivating. He focused only on the pleasure of the moment, to his female conquests that so easily capitulated without too much persuasive effort on his part. If only, even for a moment, he had applied himself, if only he had put his talents into action, he would have been able to make a good life for himself

I felt my baby growing inside me. I lived because of the baby and for it every moment of the day. My hands rested on my belly, and I would feel a light motion, a slight stir, a little butterfly that vibrated at the touch of my fingers.

What a strange family I had. I lived in my parents' house with a child like husband who came and went. In his family he was the only brother among five sisters. His father had died young, and his mother survived via various efforts especially in not disturbing the tranquility and recklessness of that one brother. I am certain that his life was dominated by the huge love of his sisters and mother, an adoration that was reciprocated and fully shared.

One morning my Donatella was born. So little, so defenseless, so mine. Her father's enthusiasm lasted a short while, for she was of too tender an age to exhibit like a trophy. And in his long absences he was too busy searching for easy pleasures, with returns that were always shorter. His responsibilities were always more ephemeral. He exerted continual extortion to keep me tied to him, certainly not for love but for convenience, for by now our life together was more for show than reality.

We were a family without a foundation, a flower born without a seed. By now, separation from my marriage had become the only solution to a paradoxical cohabitation, more comic than tragic. He continued to collect romantic conquests, engagements that had the total blessing of his sisters for the sake of his happiness.

I often asked myself, and I was often asked, what it was like. I don't know! I had feelings of guilt for having chased myself into such a strange situation. But I had no recriminations, no desperate thoughts of "if I were to do it again." She was there, her little hands around my neck, so many golden curls, a plump and smiling face, with deep eyes slightly elongated upwards.

I had between my arms the only thing that never disappointed me. And we requested a separation - in reality I requested it. The judge, sunken in an armchair that was too big, blathered on in an inexpressive monotone about laws and duties. He browsed the code of law with judgments as sharp as swords.

Donatella's name was mentioned and repeated many times, it echoed in the room. And I, to try to understand at least something, concentrated on that little name. Her father and I would need to take care of her for 15 days each. I would not be able to interfere on how they kept her or where. The judge elaborately described the future life of a one year old child.

He spoke of our obligations, that one cannot destroy a marriage, that it's necessary to try, it's necessary to understand and to pardon. He closed the book of law and gave us our assignment: the requirement to have our own house, six months of real cohabitation there, and then to return to the judge. I preferred to try the cohabitation, for I knew with absolute certainty that my husband would not be able to carry through with it.

The cohabitation lasted only briefly. In less than a month I was expecting my second child. This did not influence in any way my decisions, and the separation became absolutely obvious.

I could have aborted the child, given that it was a risky pregnancy and the situation rather delicate, but I never considered the possibility of interrupting the pregnancy. I put myself under constant medical care. In my system of beliefs the word abortion does not exist.

And so then, one day, by chance, I ran into Gregorio again. He was walking, absorbed in thought, alongside his mother and aunts. He was in Sardinia for a few days again. They were coming my way.

Donatella's little hand was firmly in mine. I made a quick deviation towards the outside of the porticoes of Via Roma, my heart in tumult, trying not to lengthen my stride so as to not seem I was running. And then his voice, and the familiar dive in my heart. My only salvation was that little hand I squeezed.
"'Ciao, Piera, how are you?"

His gaze rested on Donatella. He stroked her hair for a fraction of a second, time enough for me to unfurl the most artificial and chilly smile possible.

"Ciao, I am well, this is Donatella."

I went on to talk to him about her, her little face pointed towards us with an air of curiosity and wonder.

"I am happy for you, you have everything that you deserve, a happy family, and I hope. a husband you love."

The indissolubility of marriage…with beautiful words I painted my life as tranquil and full, without ever looking him in the eye.

Then a handshake, and he said goodbye, wishing for me a serene existence.

I walked as if in a dream. My eyes burned a bit, perhaps it was the wind or perhaps not. I had avoided telling him I was expecting a child, I only listened. I avoided telling him that I had been separated for several months, I didn't want to let him know about my failed marriage.

To survive I took refuge often in my past dream. I tasted the torture of solitary walks in the botanical garden, the plants were always the same with their lofty names, but I was alone. I no longer had Gregorio's hand which squeezed mine, his tranquil voice that explained the various species, his sweet and entertained gaze, that tangible sense of sure protection.

I was on my own and I focused all my love on my babies. The future was rarely mentioned, it was absolutely foggy. I took each day as it came. Tomorrow one would see. And then Daniela was born, wondrously beautiful. And mine, only mine.

I was always near my parents and my siblings. Attico was protective and always present. A few hours after the birth, which was long and painful, a warmth enveloped me, the baby there next to me. I sank into a deep sleep.

I heard my name barely whispered, a dream too often repeated, a light pressure on my hair, I slowly opened my eyes. Gregorio was there, real. I stretched out my hand and met his. He went over to the cradle, he pried open with a finger the little hand tenaciously closed in a fist. He smiled, and from that moment in the bottom of my heart I gave to Daniela the papà she didn't have.

"Piera, why didn't you tell me anything? Why did you pretend to be content and happy, why? I would have continued to fight for us...maybe I would have won. Now it is too late, too late..."

And then in the morning, a little bouquet of violets was there as testimony that it was all true.

By means of quick exchanges of information, tickets of typical congratulations, and news picked up here and there, I learned that he was getting married. He had accepted a marriage, love and business, a union of assured success. He finally had taken back the family business and his life.

My life had become an existence based on a routine of work. News of him that arrived to me was sometimes pungently pleasurable, and other times it reaffirmed that fairy tales and dreams are always unattainable. But that dream for me was life itself, guarded scrupulously in my heart.

And so, one day fell behind another. I had infinite love for Dona and Dani and the regret of not being able to enjoy them fully. The daytime seemed endless, but in the evenings I squeezed them in my arms, feeling their little hearts beating in unison with mine. Every act, thought, and project was bound tightly to them. They were mine, and mine only.

LETTERS

I began to receive some letters from Gregorio. At first formal, then little by little more sincere, more personal. From every word shone forth a heartbreaking melancholy, a regret for things never truly experienced, the physical and moral need to find some peace.

He was living once again in the great house, trying desperately to forget. Every day he saw again the same people that had caused so much pain to him and above all to his family. Rebuilding on still smoking ruins was proving to be ever more tiresome.

I would wait for his letters, trying to hold at bay my emotions. I would respond with specific descriptions of my days, which were fairly basic and uninteresting chronicles.

A theme we avoided at all costs was our past love. Any hint of our dreams or of our love became almost a game of strategic assessment. I was convinced that the brief period of our love, a fundamental experience of my life, had been for him instead a summer fling and nothing more.

I dressed myself fully in the guise of a good friend. In friendly letters, I encouraged him to create his own family, his own children, a life that was only his. His responses were never very clear or convincing, just subtle hints about his life in the little town, his friends, and their excursions to Orvieto.

It was as if he had put armor around his emotions and his heart. I discovered a man I didn't know before. He lived day to day, he had forgotten the past, and the future lived only until the evening. Sometimes I had a desire to probe this apathetic way. But I was afraid. I dreaded discovering who this person truly was, if he was different from the one whom I was imagining and whom I was thinking of. And if after all, I had simply been a summer fling.

Would I need to demolish piece by piece the dream of my great love, which had been the sanctuary of my life? Egoistically I agreed to fulfill the role of being at least a good friend.

Time passed relentlessly, marked only by the anguish of letters that were always the same, faithful copies one after the other. And so the demolition work began. Of the words eternal love, I eliminated eternal and what remained was the conviction of a love lived as an end in itself, it didn't matter if it had been for only a minute, it didn't matter if it was one-way. What counted was that it had been lived, that I lived it still. To imagine myself tight within the arms of a man I loved with all of my being. Without but and without why, I wanted to taste that moment as if it were my last, to relive it all the way until the end of my life.

I began to weave my canvas. The letters began to take on a different tone. Little allusions, phrases spoken and unspoken, memories always clearer and more unambiguous of our brief past together, responses always anchored to a programmed resistance. Then the revelation.

He declared to me, or better yet he acknowledged, his great love for me which was unchanged. I was his only reason for living. But in his situation nothing had changed. He had the same pressures for a marriage of convenience. His life was full of work, and of guilt for being, even if indirectly, the reason and cause for the ruin of his family.

Suddenly after this desperate confession the letters stopped. Not a hint, not a word. An unnerving and painful wait, a bottomless void.

And then unexpectedly, I was offered a trip to the continent. My brother Franco was an officer in the army, stationed in Foligno. I could go and visit him.

I shed any remaining hesitancy, threw my pride to the sea, and in little over an hour I removed all the convictions, resistance, and principles that had been cemented over the years. I had the knowledge finally that I would have the right to a parenthesis of a life that was all mine.

PIERA RETURNS TO THE CONTINENT

I sent a telegram securing the time and day of our meeting. Strangely, unlike some of my letters, this was delivered. I went with my brother to see a film. I visited the military barracks, I shook many hands. My heart was in turmoil with the fear that Gregorio might not come, the dread of being deluded again or worse, a wound to my pride, that there would be no future hopes for me, no eternal love or realization of dreams.

I would have liked to have told Franco not to leave me alone. I continued to pin him down with childish and banal questions about his work, to which he gave responses that I didn't hear. Then I said goodbye to Franco. I returned to the hotel with my gaze focused on the floor. The handle of my purse became an anchor of salvation as I waited. Then that voice, unique and unmistakeable.

"You are here, I was afraid you wouldn't come," he said. And in a crazy whirling of fears and emotions, I raised my eyes. He was there, in front of me, his caressing gaze, the golden flashes of his eyes that heated my heart. Everything fell away and a golden cloud surrounded us. Everything dissolved, the lost years, the suffering, the waits, the neglected possibilities. He and I were there together, to give life to a new dream.

We had some unforgettable days, expectations I never even dreamed of. We didn't talk about tomorrow, only today existed. His kisses and caresses fell in a crescendo of emotions that have rendered those moments eternal.

I returned to Sardinia, a one hour flight. My joy made me stop breathing. Everything seemed to me to celebrate my love. The blue of the sea, the clouds that seemed like they were escorting the flight. Light and fluttering they cradled a reality even more beautiful than the dream, a little whispering sealed by kisses: "Wait for me, I am coming back."

His letters were now more frequent, their tones different. Full of so much love, so much regret. It was as if a dam had suddenly burst into an unstoppable flood of things never forgotten...our meetings at the tidal pool or insignificant occurrences became important from the force of mentally recalling them.

But everything was still difficult. His brief visits, the need for us to hide due to possible threatening injustice from the man was still my husband. The process of the separation was long and taxing, they required from me a behavior that was more than pristine, there was the continual threat of taking Dona and Dani away from me. This threat pervaded our lives, it represented a danger. The paternal instinct is innate from birth, you have it or you don't. It is something that Gregorio demonstrated every day, brimming full of protection, love, the sense of responsibility, feelings and ways of being foreign to revenge or vendettas.

We tasted and savored little drops of hope, and finally my marriage separation was legally permitted. My children were legally mine.

The forbidden world began to gradually give way, little cracks that let us glimpse a future reality of a world that had once had rejected me.

ACCEPTANCE

An invitation to dinner at his parents' house arrived. I accepted with reserve. I was afraid of not being calm enough, or not being ready. Perhaps I would not be capable of passing an exam I had previously taken and failed without appeal.

Gregorio was calm and assured. With a vaguely teasing smile he said, "I will stay close to you, I won't let them eat you!"

The big day arrived. I wanted to be beautiful, so I dressed with particular care. I tried not to imagine that my beauty could help me avoid a war, or even soften their steadfastness. I also tried to overlook that their motives of opposition and refusal might truly be crushing and severe. I had two daughters and a failed marriage behind me.

In the end there was no need to worry. I found in them understanding and friendliness, a hardly concealed request of forgiveness for having made us suffer, for not having understood the depth of our feelings.

And so I set out into my fairy tale: a family. Even if it wasn't a legal family, it was without doubt a family in an embryonic stage.

The time came when the door of the great house in Umbria was finally opened to me, the house that had been both dream and nightmare of my past.

Gregorio came to pick me up at Fiumicino airport, he hugged me and said "Come on, let's go home." Unfamiliar landscapes, never before seen under the influence of a joy so profound. My heart was beating, punctuating an uncontrollable cry, "Home, home!"

There in the distance was Orvieto, suspended between heaven and earth, an island of beauty. It was a treasure chest that guarded thousand year old beautiful things, like the Duomo, a human miracle, erected by divine hands, a challenge and contest of the beauty that was created.

We continued past Orvieto along an unpaved road. There were a few houses around the train station, and not far away was the bridge above the Paglia river. Its arches stood out against the sky, remembering tragic events from the recent war, bombings and so many human lives wasted uselessly.

With difficulty, the car began to climb light ascents surrounded between forests. In the distance were hills striped with a myriad of clay ravines. The grays of the clay were gray wounds between the green of the meadows, a clay seemed to conquer the green.

I was a bit worried for the curving road seemed neverending. Then came a short straight-away and up high a little town that stuck out against the sky. The town seemed almost to ask forgiveness from the forests and the countryside. Its form, its harmony with the houses castled together, one next to the other, represented a hymn to the beauty of the countryside, an invitation to stop, to admire the marvelous panorama.

A piazza, the town hall. I tried to scrunch down into my seat and I closed my eyes as the car passed under the arched gateway of the town, its side squeaked against the narrow wall. I turned, but no, the car was still intact - and also the wall.

A few meters further on we reached a narrow alley. The car stopped, and there was the great house with its haughty front door, presumptuous and very aware of its role. It is difficult to describe what my state of mind was, I was to enter into a place I had only imagined and conjured based on my reveries, in fanciful daydreams.

The great house, its history...I imagined it full of happy festivity, then invaded and sacked by hate and resentment. For me it represented a forbidden paradise.

Slowly you opened the front door. The beating of my heart was strangling me, I wasn't able to see anything clearly. I smelled a scent of oldness and of abandonment, but you were there.

A while marble staircase, surrounded on all sides by frescoed walls. I climbed the stairs slowly, the sound of my steps seemed to forcefully invade a place that had rejected me, but you were there.

You turned, a smile mixed with amusement and teasing. You understood my fears, my hesitations. You took me in your arms, my face resting on your chest, the roughness of your jacket... I had thought that never in my life would I be able to feel that sense of joy and fulfillment. My remaining feelings of guilt disappeared, replaced by the awareness that one minute can be enough to fill a whole life.

We entered into the formal living room and you brought me back to earth with, "Piera you are home."

Your arm squeezed my waist. There was no longer the oppressive odor of a being closed, of being old, but a jubilation of colors. The blue of the walls were vivid with shoots of roses. I wanted to pass my hands on those sagging and tired damask silks, to imprint on my mind those colors, that perfume of past eras, to capture in myself that moment, to savor the knowledge of an unknown world.

Tears gushed from my eyes, and you caressed my hair. "Don't cry, love, we will make the splendor of this house be reborn again, this is our house."

A FAMILY

We began our life together, you, I, Donatella and Daniela. We were a family not in the eyes of the law but respected and loved by all. We had happy days together. I felt I was wife and mother in every sense of those titles. But there was a little sharpened thorn in the bottom of my heart, the suffering for being in a situation at the edge of legality.

Everyone embraced me, understood me, perhaps loved me, but the sense of guilt was there nonetheless, stinging and painful.

After a few years of living together, I found myself expecting a child. It is difficult to speak of the joy considering our irregular social position and a continued, unnerving wait for a divorce that was slow to arrive. The mysterious path ahead of how we might marry...I was full of pain and fear. But you were there, you softened my suffering, you calmed me and I abandoned myself to the irrepressible joy of Dona and Dani. They were expecting a little brother, they were too small to be smothered by laws that were savage and heartless.

When the birth drew near, we decided to ask the advice of a priest, symbol of Christian understanding and piety. We left the house in close formation, you, I, and the girls. You were rather skeptical that the priest might be able to understand our situation. But I counted very much on the serenity of our family unit. We were already that which we wanted to be, a family.

The priest listened to my story. I told him everything. I didn't want forgiveness, or absolution. I just wanted that my baby would not be born with sin that wasn't his fault, that he would not be condemned for a fault that wasn't his.

The priest responded In a calm and persuasive voice. He avoided our eyes and his diaphanous hand tinkered around the desktop.

"Signora, you are an inexcusable sinner. You force these innocent creatures to live in your sin, and then you bring another child into this world without any point of reference, without a future."

As I reeled from the shock of his words, he illustrated abundantly and in detail how we could save our souls. I would need to immediately entrust Dona and Dani to a healthy environment and there they would be redeemed of the sin. The baby about to be born would need to be put in an orphanage, for adoption.

Up until that point, Gregorio had not spoken. I had painstakingly avoided looking at him. Daniela was anchored at his side. With his hand on the door handle, Gregorio asked, "And then?"

The priest looked at him. "Then, since you are an unmarried man you can request to adopt the baby. Pray to God that in adopting He will forgive you. If God instead decides that other parents will have the baby, try to atone and to conceive another child within the grace of a real, sanctified family."

We left, not defeated, not destroyed. But aware that sometimes God can make a mistake - in this case in the choice of his representative on earth.

We challenged everything and everyone and on July 31, 1966, Momi was born. A lock of blonde hair, blue eyes, a little being with a strong determination and will to live.

But it wasn't easy. We had so much suffering. Momi was given mistaken treatments and approximate diagnoses. His life was tied to a thin thread. Many sleepless nights, many prayers. Gregorio and I took shifts holding him in our arms, walking him around, his little face always more emaciated, his hands always more delicate. How I prayed!

I offered up my life of sin, my happiness won with such diffi-culty, in exchange for that little life. I lost at times my faith in God, I refused however to think of Him vindictively. Often I begged Him, invoked Him, and He was there.

And then finally the nightmare was over. Momi took his first steps, and we had the certainty that the worst was behind us. To see my baby bloom again, day after day, was a miracle. His loved his sisters and was also despot and dictator. Donatella is still today for him a sense of maternal protection and infinite love.

He had a cheery smile and also sudden dark moods, his little hands wrapped around his Papà's neck. He was the joy of his grandparents. Paradise was in the blue of his eyes...the baby we had always dreamed of.

You and I, Dona, Dani, Momi. Our love is there to savor in every moment as if it were the last. But suffering in the bottom of my heart reminded me... do I deserve all this wonder?

I prayed that all that we had achieved would last as long as pos-sible. There were years peppered with joys and pains. There was the death of your mother, Ada, who I had known for just a short time. She was so delicate in a world that she didn't understand. There were events for which she had not been prepared, like her new expanded family. She was a woman imprisoned in her iron religious rigidity. She never forgave herself for not having understood how great my love was for her son. I loved her and I took care of her.

When Ada was dying, the priest came to give her last rites and hear her confession. The priest administered communion to Ada and then turned to give me communion as well. I shook my head and said, "No, I can't, I'm separated."
Ada turned to the priest and said, "Piera is separated because of me, because of my actions. It's not her fault. Take that sin from

her and put it on me."
And this priest gave me communion.

I would have never attributed my suffering to Ada. Because I could not regret anything of my ill-chosen first marriage - from that union Dona and Dani were born. I lavished on them the best of me, I remember them with Grandfather Momo, Gregorio's father. The image is carved into my mind, he was in his wheelchair, smiling with Dona perched on one armrest, and Dani on the other, with Momi held in his arms.

Grandfather Momo's laugh was everywhere, festive and contagious. He lived in his world where the past trumped the present. It became a battle between reality and fantasy. He would call me over and indicate the stark little piazza in front of the house, "Look at the grain, it is not beautiful, look how it waves like a blue green sea." The only green I saw was a little tree in a continual struggle for survival. But he looked at me ecstatically. He didn't always know who I was, but I was there and I shared with him his joy.

Suddenly his gaze would darken, his eyes searched past the door, "Ada where are you?"

She had been his lifetime companion, the small, delicate woman who at his side had been devastated by events she endured that were not her fault.

He would look at me then. I represented one of his few points of reference in a world that played hide and seek with his mind. Here a memory, a landscape, a face. Now his mind was populated only by uncertain figures never clearly delineated, fluctuating in a reality that he was not able to grasp, a reality that was shifty and elusive.

I was there and he would ask me, "But Ada, where is she?"

I would lean over toward the brake of the baby carriage so as to hide that I was drying my tears. I straightened the tartan blanket on his lap. I fussed about and bought time as I tried to find the most possibly believable response.

"Don't worry, soon Ada will be back. For now I am here for you."

His eyes became calm again in a glimmer of logic, and smiling he looked at me. "Better it's you! In the exchange I definitely made out for the better!"

His eyes shone, a light resurgence of past times and witty jokes. His fingers unraveled with meticulous calm the fringe of his tartan blanket. The past, present, and today evaporated in a gentle rain of colored threads that in a last delicate flight scattered themselves at his feet.

And one day he rejoined his Ada. I like to think of them there together, in a world that I hope is better. So much happiness held in check by that sharpened point that often, in betrayal, pierces your heart. Your family, there they are, your whole world is there.

The divorce, for reasons of obstruction on the part of my first husband, progressed and then receded in a cruel and perverse game. Documents came back to us without signature. The man who was my husband specialized in a painful game, appearing, disappearing, threatening in an unnerving and upsetting way. He was full of Yes today and No tomorrow.

But all this did not crush our hopes, instead it reinforced our love and our steely determination. Never even for a minute did we think about our union with suffering, or about our uncertain legal position, but only about our life, that which was lived minute by minute with infinite love. Our love gave us the certainty that only death would be able to separate us.

We passed marvelous days at the seaside, you and I hand in hand, almost incredulous to really be there together. Dona and Dani chased each other, trying to include Momi in the games. You gave them their first swimming lessons, your strong arm supporting them, they were enveloped by a feeling of trust and security.

In the distance, Cagliari with its lights tried to earn first prize in a competition for the most beautiful. But it had too many rivals - Villasimius, the beach at La Maddalena, Chia and Capo Teulada. In every cove the sea changed with a thousand reflections, it played with the sun, becoming here even purplish, there dark, it caressed the bank transforming the waves in graceful crowns of foam, lace hems frothing that no human hand could recreate, always and forever. For a moment the sand is adorned with the waves, then lets them go. You know they will come back, sometimes furious, sometimes calm, but they will come back.

Time passed slowly and times changed, That which is certain today is no longer here tomorrow. Momi was six years old, Dona e Dani were growing up, and I was expecting another baby.

For the first time in my life, I experienced a pregnancy with unbounded joy and peace. I showed my belly off with serene pride, I wanted to forget the difficult walks during my pregnancy with Momi every night, fearful that some morally imperious soul would see me, that someone could assert false rights over a baby that was ours only.

Times had changed significantly since then. I obtained in 1972 the legal separation based on guilt of my ex-husband. Even divorce was near. They were wonderful months of my pregnancy, a love always truer and deeper, and that suffering in the bottom of my heart always, always less painful.

After various false alarms, on May 14, 1973, Arrigo was born. The miracle of love was here in my arms. Gregorio caressed his little hands, looked at him incredulously, ecstatic. Arrigo was tight against me, squirming, a little rebel, fearless. He decreed his clear differentiation from his siblings who were all blonde, almost all bald, while he boasted a wild head of hair that was decisively raven black.

His chubby little face and dark eyes were illuminated by a thousand golden flecks. He too was so tiny, so defenseless. In just a few minutes he commanded the total capitulation of the whole family, adults and children, and appointed his siblings as his security detail.

Dona received the news that her little brother had been born while she was at school. There was a mutiny attempt, the teachers were overpowered by an enthusiasm never seen before. Dani, still little, participated marginally. The baby was too young to play with, so she figured she would wait for better times to decide whether to get excited or not.

Momi, curious, studied the infant in all the smallest details. Arrigo was tiny, and he screamed, but the most absolutely unforgivable thing for Momy was that baby Arrigo didn't have any teeth.

Between Gregorio and I, a fierce and, I think, unjustified rivalry broke out. Gregorio would come home early, anticipating to the exact second the time to give Arrigo a bath. I was tired, and Gregorio would take over.

Gregorio would get up during the night and change the baby. And so I remained essential only for nursing, reasons absolutely and fortunately immutable. Gregorio experienced fatherhood for the first time with full delight, without fear and without the need to give all of his weight and understanding to me. In those other times we were so afraid of a thousand problems of my situation, a situation that was anomalous to say the least.

MARRIAGE

Then the day came. November 19, 1974, a Piera radiant and cheerful burst from the front door, exploding with happiness. My step was confident and my hair was tossed in the wind as I held tight to the arm of the only man I had ever loved.

Dressed extremely elegantly, your hair lightly streaked with gray at the temples, you were there, your gaze warm, the touch of your hand reassuring and confident as always.

My heart performed daunting acrobatics, unleashed from the reason that was inviting it to be calm. Our destination was the town hall of Cagliari, its white spires showing off their splendid brightness. Flocks of birds twirled in countless dances woven between sky and sea.

The wind in the branches of the fabulous magnolia tree and on its dancing papyrus bushes improvised my wedding march. My hand was tight in yours, my haven, consolation, and hope for the future.

The mayor of Elmas knew our whole story. He adjusted the sash around his chest. He was nervous, but beat back his emotion. Mine was just whispered, and yours is the echo whispered so many years ago.

Our signatures. Then I descended the stairs floating a meter above earth. The air was brighter, the wind ruffled my hair, your hand, your gaze...what had changed?

I was your body and soul, and now everything was legal. My thoughts flew to all the past years. There on the banks of the tidal pool at Elmas I gave you my soul, and afterward I didn't have it myself anymore. One can't live without a spirit. The air was truly clearer now, the birds twirled weightlessly, you were near me and I know with absolute certainty that God was always near me too.

And the pain in my heart was gone.

THE FAMILY RETURNS TOGETHER TO THE CONTINENT

Years followed of pure and total happiness. A future of remaining in Sardinia that had seemed certain began to vacillate, There was need to return to Umbria, to the great house. We were a bit apprehensive. But the world was there to start again. Dona and Dani were dismayed that they would need to leave behind their grandparents, cousins, life long friends, their childhood, everything that had been a part of their world.

I tried to describe to them their new town, I stressed its high points, with the promise of returning soon to Sardinia. The preparation for the move was meticulous so as to not have time to think too much about it. I made a point every night of watching the sunset. I wanted to imprison in my eyes that dazzling splendor of fiery rays in the waves, rays that gave them a luminosity and transparency that wasn't real.

The day of departure arrived. I wandered around our house, a house now desolately empty. So many memories emerged. I smiled and bolstered myself. Then the ship slowly left the pier. Briefly the sharp taste of rust mixed with the briny sea propelled me a thousand light years back in time. Then I pushed back my childhood into the meanderings of my memory.

In the distance there were two specks on the pier, my parents. Mamma, with a scarf in her hand tried to seem festive to the children, an orange waving that my tears obscured and pained me until finally they disappeared.

Upon our arrival in Allerona, among the townspeople arose a curiosity mixed with indifference. They did not know me very well. I had been there only irregularly for a few days at a time, and they had never seen Dona and Dani. But they were informed of their existence and eager to see them. Sardinian girls - they imagined them like the prototype of a tiny Sardinian woman with black hair and olive skin.

The little road was alive with people for there was so much novelty - the door of the great house was ajar and the windows open wide. Now slowly the car door opened, and their curiosity reached emotional peaks.

First appeared Dona, tall and blonde, stunningly beautiful - I beg your forgiveness for saying so but she was. A union of grace and harmony. Then Dani with her cascade of blond curls, velvety eyes, her elegant feminine step, it was difficult to find in her any flaw as she was practically perfect. In just a few minutes the old ideas and misconceptions about the beauty of Sardinian women were annihilated.

Our new environment was of stunning countryside landscapes, extending endlessly to centuries old forests. Little towns castled on hills of various altitudes, a soft and sly nostalgia that was hard to eradicate. But my family was there, the world I had created with so much difficulty.

I was a foreigner in a town that I should have felt was mine. I felt a little splinter of granite carried to me with the wind, a wind imbued by the sea with the sweet perfume of the eucalyptus trees. I felt in my core that I was Sardinian. With pride I declared that my children were Sardinian, they were born there and because of that they were Sardinian by divine will.

I gave in to little sporadic daydreams. I was diving into the blue of the sea, below the long rows of prickly pear bushes decorated with flowers as yellow as the sun. The flowers seemed unaware of the threatening thorns on the pears. I could taste their fragrant and juicy fruit.

The sunsets down there towards the tidal pool, the jolting movements of the leaping fish, the seagulls' flights...

But slowly I came back to reality. I heard your voice calling me. I put away my daydream of Sardinia and her delights and I closed it in an angle of my heart.

This dream of mine, of my life, is tied to you, that beautiful island, it is cloaked in sweet and melancholy poetry, day after day.

We were very busy in those days, Gregorio and I. We tried to remove or at least lessen all the unpleasant scarring that the great house had undergone. We wanted to restore it, if not to its past splendors, then at least to the pleasant comfortable dwellings of a happy family.

Our enthusiasm was infused with joy. We decided it was best to preserve the wallpaper as much as possible with the original colors and forms. We refreshed it with new vital nourishment all that had been covered by a melancholy aging lacquer. At first the painted flowers and colonnades of the old paper refused to collaborate, almost resigned to their deteriorated state.

But after so much work, in the end our perseverance rewarded us. The colonnades, the roses shone with the rays of the sun, they came to life and a little of the old splendor reemerged. We added to the windows curtains that fluttered, full of life. So much work! But that old air, of something extinguished, of something that had declined irreversibly, was gone.

With the joyous voices of the children as well as our own exuberance, the great house finally had a twitch of a proud comeback. The sun no longer ignored it. Our love illuminated it with new passion, and it returned almost to its old glories. Happiness became palpable in every angle, and the future seemed full of rosy certainty.

GREGORIO'S ILLNESS

The battles against a visible enemy were over, a triumph over bureaucracy and Italian laws all too clear and too imprecise at the same time. Yet just around the corner was the *invisible* enemy, that which attacked Gregorio physically one day, wearing down his spirits. He tried to understand why.

You started off like that. Strong pains zapped your strength. You began long stays in the hospital. I tried to divide my time between your sickbed and home. Dona grew up fast for her new responsibilities in my absence. How many sleepless nights we had, I stayed close to you until deep into the night, and then you would send me home. "Piera, go home, I will be ok."

Your face was always more pinched, your hands always weaker. I exhorted you to resist. I showed you I was strong and confident, sure of myself, but it was a difficult to feign. I was never sure that you would not see my desperation.

Late at night I would return home. The road I used to take in your company I drove alone now. It seemed endless. My eyes were full of tears, a continual talk with God, prayers, begging, blackmail, I asked for a little extension, a few more days of serenity.

Then between the fog and the tears would appear our little town. I had just a few meters to wipe out the tears, to put my face back together in an expression of false tranquility. I climbed the stairs with a sure step, forcing the will of my legs that protested.

And there they were, all leaning on the balustrade. Dona held in her arms tightly Arrigo, Dani squeezed Momi's hand. I smiled,

"It's ok, children, it will be ok, Papà sends his love, and soon he will come home. Go to bed."

The flames danced in the fireplace. Dona looked at me silently, and asked no questions.

The next morning the road was still the same, but this time it seemed too short. I wished it would never end, I was afraid to arrive. I dreaded how I might find you, if I would find you. The last stretch before I reached you was a long and steep flight of stairs, and then your room, the one reserved for those who are hopeless, a place where prayers pile up on one another and shatter from the force.

I placed my foot on the first step. I felt empty, I wiped away the last tear. I looked up to see the smiling face of Sister Vincenza peeking out and beckoning me to come up. You were alive and you were expecting me. I flew up the stairs to your door and you were there, your weak hand caressed my face, my poor love, a whisper just hinted and my hope reignited. I made peace with God, and I prayed.

We had days of highs and lows, nights with no sleep, doctors visits. For the first time it was I who made the decisions, I unearthed a Piera who was strong, determined and deciseful. I was grateful that my life thus far had forged me into what I became.

I was grateful for Sister Vincenza, a little ghost of goodness and understanding. Always present, she put a stop to my desperate crying. An ally, she kept me informed, and she urged me to never give up hope.

One morning I arrived to find Gregorio particularly quiet, his eyes stubbornly closed. He was tired. Even Sister Vincenza seemed strangely silent, fearful. I tried to understand why. She finally said that that morning Gregorio had requested communion.

I struggled to understand why, knowing his difficult relationship with the clergy based on past experiences. I thought of how great his gratitude to God was, yet how aware he might be to death.

The priest had entered dressed in his presumptuous robes despite not being worthy of them. He was proud of his power, triumphant in his authority. Having listened to Gregorio's confession, he simply turned on his heels and left. I was divorced, I was a sinner and Gregorio had lived with me. He was not worthy to receive forgiveness.

The priest left but God remained there under the closed eyes of Gregorio, and never abandoned him.

My view of the clergy underwent a strong blow. Certainly my dedication as a church goer isn't a good example. But after that, I set up a direct dialogue with God, a privileged line. I saw God in the flowers, in the flight of the butterflies, in my children's eyes. I thanked Him for the life He had given me, for the good and for the bad.

I speak with God, and I never doubt that He knows everything about me. I observe often the immensity of the heavens. Perhaps He doesn't always have much time to listen to me, but everything that I have had in my life confirms to me that He is there and He hears me.

My visits to Gregorio were a succession of alternating phases. He had long stays in various hospitals. Some hopeful periods, fearful periods, even little periods of good health. But all too little to be free of fear.

Then, not because I aspired to, but for the fact that I was physically stronger, I began to undercut the primacy of Gregorio without intending to. Between operations, hospital stays, recoveries and relapses, I saw his weakness in facing his illness, and his desperate and disarming fragility compared to my strength. I became strong, for him and for me. I was aware that if he were to notice my despairing weakness, he would have given up.

I learned to make that which was not normal seem normal, even when I knew it was perfectly useless. He had to follow the rules and have a normal life and routine, but I found it was useless to say things like, "Don't smoke, it's bad for you. Try to walk instead."

He would respond, "I'm tired."

To which I would say, "No, you are lazy."

I would push the wheelchair, looking at his hands tapered and stretched out to find some warmth that wasn't there. I felt those hands tightly against my body, firm, alive, hard, affectionate, their light touch on my hair, my hair that he loved so much.

The nape of his neck was so delicate, I wanted to stroke his face with my hands, to put my body next to his and infuse him with even a little of my warmth, but I couldn't. He lived because I lived, and any demonstration of weakness would have seemed a surrender. I had to convince him that everything was normal, and just a question of time.

I urged him to walk, little steps at my side over to his studio, over to browse the things that he loved so much, the antique keepsakes, remembrances of a time not too long ago. His gaze quickly found the photographs, characters of a world that no longer existed. Sometimes it was too painful to remember.

"I'm tired", he would say. And I would smile, summoning a normality that didn't exist.

"You're not tired, you're lazy." He would look at me rapturously. I walked for him, I lived for him, I was his strength, I was his life.

For me, he learned to pretend, "You will see, Piera, I will get better, we will still go to see so many beautiful places, we will climb up Mortirolo, we will find the little red house, that point of reference for the fearless young soldiers."

Hovering on the edge of the orthopedic bed, I kissed him. He took my hands and returned my kiss, he asked my forgiveness. I fought back tears, forgiveness for what? Forgiveness for not being any more what he had been at one time, and his accidental rigidness of the past. I had nothing to forgive. I smiled, the last effort of normalcy, of a hope that had ended long ago.

Then came the nights that never ended, the pillow soaked from my tears, the smothered hiccups. My hand that sought his, stretched out to feel his breath, every time he called me. I was there with you, until your last breath.

It is an infinite night that you live every day.

We began our dream ten years late, years that were canceled by a reality never even dreamed of, never imagined. We had an infinite love, overflowing, capable of eliminating distances, the awareness that every moment together would have dissolved the lost years, the physical and spiritual pain. And so passed those many years.

In my whole life you maintained every promise, except the one of never leaving me alone.

I am here. You left me three years ago. My thoughts fly to you in every moment, I see you as you were, determined and proud.

Where are you? Your fellow soldiers, many of them went before you. They are there with you, of that I am certain. They are aware and grateful of your meticulous research work, you were fastidious, focused on reuniting the survivors, to organize those first reunions. You gave them back their fiery bravado from when they were twenty years old, you revitalized memories buried in the bottom of your heart, the integrity of having been the flower of Italian youth and the pride of having lived as protagonists in a mythical and unrepeatable era.

Thank you for having given me the privilege of fusing my life with yours. Thank you for your absolute and total love. Always in your heart I was the first and only claimant, and I am proud to be so.

I am here, in our house, even though now I occupy just a little part of it. Solitude is a subtle and treacherous evil. Suddenly it assails me and suffocates me, my eyes fill with tears. The days march one after the other in search of a memory, or of a little particular detail that was left out, and which has now become important for a mosaic of a million pieces that fit together, among each other, and become the past.

I slowly climb the stairs. The years weigh like boulders, in stark contrast with my free thoughts, full of ideas. The freedom of these ideas are in opposition with my legs which are always less sturdy.

Then one day, like the rest of the days difficult but always the prelude to evening, there is my new room, a light creaking, I hear you in the soft whisper of the wind, I look at your photograph, you are here, you take me by the hand, the door opens slowly, here is the living room a joy of blues and soft colors, the columns come to life, the flowers grace us with their colors, I brush with my hand the marble console, a jingling accompanies the sparks of light that shine in the mirror.

Here is the little entrance where so many years ago you took my in your arms, I feel again under my cheek the roughness of your jacket, your voice creaking with emotion, "My love, you are home, in our home, here in every angle we will live and nothing and no one will be able to wipe out our presence."

In every angle our love was able to make the house live again. The phoenix soars in infinite skies. My worries and waits for you to come home. The tractor climbs and descends the slopes in a slow rhythm, monotone, my gaze anchored on the headlights that light up the clods of earth newly disturbed. My heart is there and tries to penetrate your love for the earth, which I will never be able to do.

The little informal dining room, the fire crackling in the hearth.

Dona, the flames dance on her hair, her eyes full of nostalgia, regret for all that she had left behind, ripe regret, memories still alive and palpable.

Dani, so cheerful, lost in dreams perhaps never fully realized.

Momi, taciturn, in a continual and bloody war between what he is and what he would like to be.

Arrigo, tirelessly lined up on the carpet his pacific soldiers, forcing us all to do fantastic maneuvers as we passed so that they are not annihilated.

You look at me and squeeze my hand, your gaze caresses me, I would like to tell you how much I love you but I feel suffocated from a sense of guilt. I loaded you with a huge responsibility and I can give you so little.

We stay a moment on the balcony, looking up at the sky dotted with stars. The stars, each one you taught me, their lofty names that seem too important for tiny spots of light, the moon our only ally for many years, every night, wherever we were, our gazes unite there in the luminosity of the evening.

Here is our room, the bed that is too big, my body tight against yours, your hand caressing my hair, softening my stresses, and dissolving my fears. You wiped out my regrets for not having a legitimate situation.

On the frescoed ceiling the little dances of the angels brush against the blue sky in an eternal pose, like a sigh. The long scarf, light and fluttery, strokes its graceful body, red coral crowns wind together one with the other, delightfully, the knots of love, the tassels seem to tremble in the air.

Now we go back into that which is now my room, and you will

leave me alone, another day without end and then the night. I know that you will come back tomorrow and then again the day after, until the day that together, hand in hand, we will be together, the last hint of your presence, the bedcovers cling to my body, lightly.

Sleep is slow to come, I think about you in the last days of your life, the anguish is always the same. It is not true that time heals the pain, for my pain is here, the distress, the regrets and sense of guilt, the only little parenthesis is the thought that soon you will come to take me away.

I see your hands again, your tapered fingers tightly seeking a heat that wasn't there, I feel again those lively hands that touched my body, strong, hard, and caressing, the light touch on my hair, on my bare skull stripped of hair due to a tumor, my hair you loved so much.

I see you again, your head slightly reclined, your neck so delicate, I would like to rest my hands on your face, lay myself next to you, infuse you with my heart, lose myself in your cold.

You squeeze my arm. "I'm tired".

I smile, "No, you are lazy." He looks at me ecstatically, amused.

"You will see, Piera, I will get better…"

I want to cry, but I smile, "Come on, let's go to sleep, tomorrow you will feel better." You point to me your side of the big bed, but I move my index finger back and forth.

"My love, you can't, you know, you need to sleep here instead," and I point to the orthopedic bed, by now absolutely indispensable for his condition.

You look at me, his face is overcast now, let down, and I whisper, "Tomorrow."

I raise the protective side of the bed, there is the orange blanket,

a present from Donatella.
You ask me to cover you with it, I check to see if your gloves are put on well so your hands stay warm.

"Sleep, I am here next to you, if you reach out your arm toward the edge of the bed you can even touch me."

The orthopedic bed edge is too high, but I stick myself out, balancing, for a goodnight kiss. With a little smile, you kiss my hands, you ask me forgiveness for your ill spells, your rigidity, perhaps for not being what you once were. But you don't have to ask me this. I caress your face and smile, the last effort to try to give a sense of security that for a long time I no longer had.

Then the night, this one longer, the pillow filled with tears, now hidden hiccups, my hand searches yours, reaches out, to feel or sense every breath or any weak call. I am with you until your last breath. You have not been able to maintain your promise of "We will die together, I will not leave you alone."

Instead, I am alone, I touch your side of the bed, it seems warm, you are with me, your photo is there. Mine is not solitude, it is as if my body is missing a limb, I live halfway, I rejoice only in part.

There, I hear the front door of my little house open slowly, it is Momy asking how I slept. He is attentive and thoughtful, that innate way of his, an endowment that wasn't learned, wasn't imposed, but born with him. The door closes again. Before long I will hear the three imperious rings of the bell, and it will be Dona. She comes to spend any moment she can with me, and leaves behind a halo of serene and confident peace, she transforms my house nto a luxurious and perfumed greenhouse.

Dani comes, too, I am never alone, I wrap myself in her love.

Arrigo, exuberant and chaotic, a thousand interests that intertwined, that pile up on each other and usually cancel themselves out. He is so physically similar to you, the same way of walking, the same rigidity, the same hidden tenderness, betrayed by the thousand gold rays that shine from his eyes. In him reemerges the tenderness and fragility, the legacy and ancient conviction of his grandmother Ada. Blood is not water.

I have a marvelous family. Often my pride makes me arrogant, but I feel authorized to put myself on a higher step.

The day of our farewell burst with sunshine. The sun warmed you with its heat, you were always so cold. The sun greeted the people who had always loved and honored you, there were many who filled up the piazza outside. A sea of flowers decorated you with a stunning Italian flag, your name echoed in the quiet reverence of the little borgo, unanimously resounded the call in the huge open valley below, "Present!". The cry bounced and traveled through the forests, the fields, and touched the expanses of grain that were still immature, and reached imposingly those highest peaks.

The flag snaps for you in the wind, and the black eagle spreads its wings, taking a high and proud flight towards the sky of a lost world, through clouds of past glories and unrepeatable hopes for certainty in a great Italy.

The black bird's flight guides you across a sky which only heroes can traverse.

Present! Forever with me.

Piera

ABOUT THE AUTHOR

Pietrina "Piera" Salvatici Misciattelli Bernardini was born in Orbetello, in Tuscany, in 1933. She grew up between Greece and Italy with her parents and three siblings. Moving frequently between these countries was fundamental for her development, but also a reason for a deep nostalgia which would never leave her. Having survived World War II with her family, she resided in Sardinia after the war. There she met the love of her life, Gregorio Misciattelli Bernardini, heir to an aristocratic Umbrian family. They were confronted, however, with the rigid social protocols of the aristocracy, which demanded for Gregorio a wife of the same social class. Piera recounts in her memoirs how the rest of their lives unfolded.

Piera lives today in Umbria with her four children, ten grandchildren, and two great-grandchildren. The family still cultivates today the family's ancient lands of wine, grain and olive oil.

OBSERVATIONS FROM THE TRANSLATOR

This is the first time that Piera's memoir has been made available to the public. It is also the first time it has ever appeared in English.

Previously, the only printed copies were in Italian, published privately for the family. It is rare that a translator has the opportunity to speak with and ask questions of the author of the original language version. I am grateful to have had this unique opportunity to work with Piera, my mother-in-law, on this project. In doing so, I have learned much more about my grandparents' native country of Italy.

This is a first edition memoir. We are planning a second expanded edition, already hand-written in Italian by Piera. The second expanded edition will fill in more detail on several of the episodes mentioned in the first edition. Not the least of these episodes is how at the end of the war Gregorio was actually saved by the Americans from their "allies" the partigiani (the partigiani who claimed to be helping the Americans but who would have murdered him.)

Apart from war scholars, few people outside of Italy know that during World War II there raged simultaneously an Italian civil war. Italy suffered greatly from this civil war. Even today, the wounds from the Italian civil war are both so deep and so recent that they are largely taboo in conversation. Italians simply cannot discuss them.

The Italian civil war divided the Italian people and the Italian armies into two opposing factions. On one side were the Fascists who remained loyal to Mussolini, and on the other side were the partisans ("partigiani") who either supported the Anglo-American effort or who wanted to ally themselves with the communist Soviets.

As a dual citizen of Italy and the United States, I reflect upon this Italian civil war of 1943 - 1945 by considering the American Civil War of 1861 - 1865. The Italian Civil War was much more recent than the American one, and in a country that was much smaller and much younger. (Despite being an ancient peninsula with ancient peoples, Italy was united as a republic only in the 1860's.) A civil war in a very small and very young country has an even stronger potential to scar its people.

Civil war is brutal. And when it is done, the victor writes the history which is then taught in schools. Americans know all too well how civil war pitted brother against brother. In America, no matter what side one "is on", it is impossible to argue that all the northern Union soldiers were saints and all the southern Confederate soldiers were demons - or vice versa.

Similarly, it is impossible to argue that all Italian "partigiani" were kind-hearted and well-intentioned, and all Fascists cruel and dangerous.

Many partisans who supported the Anglo-American and Soviet effort were indeed kind-hearted and good. And yet many partisans were also undoubtedly turncoats who changed sides once they saw how the governmental tide was turning. My own Italian family recounted how their Italian neighbors had a box of many different flags and waved the particular flag of whichever army was marching through town that day. Alliances were often made on the basis of one's best chance at survival.

Other partisans performed terrible war crimes in the name of supporting the Anglo American effort. The striking example in Piera's memoir was Rumba, who claimed to be a Robin Hood figure helping the Anglo Americans, but who actually tortured and murdered many civilians.

Surely, there were fascists who were similarly evil. But there were also countless good fascists with families who were inclusive of others and who lived by a strong moral code.

People everywhere like things to be black and white. The good side and the bad side. The good hero and the evil villain. Our wholesome protective army and their barbaric army. But things are never black and white, and this is true even more so in war. Within every human being lies the capacity for great goodness and great evil; most of us fall somewhere in the middle mix. Neither side of the war is pure and saintly.

In translating this book, I observed that many Italians who changed political coats toward the war's end chose to become communist along the Soviet model. In fact, communism is still very popular in Italy today. As Piera herself writes sardonically, after the war, "finally the people were sovereign, creators who could choose whether to be part of the satellites of Mother Russia or a colony of the Anglo American people." I can only imagine that Stalin's geographic proximity was a factor in their decision to become communist. Piera also notes seeing portraits of Stalin in the homes of communist Italians toward the end of the war.

In this memoir we have Piera's first hand accounts of what she witnessed as a child during World War II, many episodes of which have never been spoken of or printed before.

Ellen Craig Misciattelli Bernardini

FOR MORE INFORMATION

Stay informed about upcoming publications related to Piera's first edition by following our website https://www.umbriaabove.com and social media UmbriaAbove.

---

[1] https://en.wikipedia.org/wiki/Transatlantic_flight
Notable mass transatlantic flight: On 1–15 July 1933, Gen. Italo Balbo of Italy led 24 Savoia-Marchetti S.55X seaplanes 6,100 statute miles (9,800 km), in a flight from Orbetello, Italy, to the Century of Progress International Exposition Chicago, Illinois, in 47h 52m. The flight made six intermediate stops. Previously, Balbo had led a flight of 12 flying boats from Rome to Rio de Janeiro, Brazil, in December 1930 – January 1931, taking nearly a month.

[2] https://en.wikipedia.org/wiki/SS_Rex

[3] https://it.wikipedia.org/wiki/Mandracchio#/media/File:Mandraki_Harbour_-_panoramio.jpg

[4] https://it.wikipedia.org/wiki/Mandracchio#/media/File:Mandraki_Harbour_-_panoramio.jpg

[5] https://en.wikipedia.org/wiki/Colossus_of_Rhodes#/media/File:Colossus_of_Rhodes.jpg

[6] Upon a return to Rhodes in approximately 2010, the author spoke with local residents who indicated that Signor Drachidi was a collaborator or spy (depending on one's point of view) working with the Americans during the war.

[7] https://en.wikipedia.org/wiki/Italian_Social_Republic The RSI was the final attempt of Mussolini to win the war and comprised only the part of Italy from Lazio northward. Some call the RSI a German puppet state. It existed from 1943-1945.

[8] https://en.wikipedia.org/wiki/Marocchinate The author may be ref-

erencing the Marocchinate.

[9] The author recalls that this woman was the wife of a fascist, with no fascist participation herself.

[10] The author recalls that the victim had no more flesh on the tips of his fingers as the flesh had been completely worn off as he tried to hold himself up with his hands on the rough stone wall.

[11] The author states that the body of the miller's son was never found.

[12] The hammer and the sickle were the symbol of the Communist party.

[13] https://en.wikipedia.org/wiki/Sor_Pampurio Sor Pampurio was a bald cartoon character from the 1920's to the 1970's

[14] Many Italians felt that the September 1943 armistice was a betrayal of Italy.

Made in the USA
Monee, IL
20 January 2022

89459038R00138